Where Do We Go

from Here?

WHERE
DO WE GO FROM
HERE?

Harold J. Laski

1940

New York : The Viking Press : Publishers

For ROBIN

and for the millions who, like him,
are risking their lives for freedom

Contents

CHAPTER ONE

WHERE WE STAND TODAY

11

CHAPTER TWO

WHAT FASCISM IS

76

CHAPTER THREE

WHAT ARE WE TO DO NEXT?

129

CHAPTER ONE

◇◇

Where We Stand Today

I

SINCE September 3, 1939, Hitler has brought every independent country in Western Europe, with the single exception of Great Britain, under his domination. If Sweden remains formally neutral, it is only because he has, so far, decided that he does not require the advantages he might derive by overrunning it. In South-Eastern Europe, every country except Turkey and Greece lies within the ambit of his power. The Soviet Union retains, so far, its freedom of manœuvre. But it is obvious from the precautions the rulers of the Kremlin have taken to strengthen their frontiers and their defensive preparations that they place no confidence in Hitler's pledge of non-aggression. Not since Napoleon after the signature of Tilsit has the authority of any conqueror in European civilization been so widespread. Not even Napoleon achieved it with a speed as breathless. Only Great Britain stands between Hitler and a decisive empire over the whole European Continent.

On any showing, the achievement is a remarkable one. It is remarkable for the efficiency and rapidity of its execution. It is remarkable for the ease with which, above all in France, the conquered were tempted to accept their fate. It is remarkable for the completeness with which it has overthrown a way of life increasingly accepted since the French Revolution as the central objective of civilized man. It is the more remarkable in that it is certain that both the methods and the aims of Hitlerism are rejected by the vast majority of those whom it controls. Hitler's rule is that of naked power. It is built upon the ability to subject numbers to his will by a terrorism before which anything Europe has known in modern times pales into insignificance. It is pitiless, ruthless, relentless. Where it sets its foot, there, of fixed purpose, it has set out to break both the bodies and the minds of those who have been sceptical of its authority. There is clearly no limit to its ambition. Were it successfully to complete its conquest of the Old World, it is certain, if anything is certain, that it would move forward to the conquest of the New. Flushed with the immense triumphs it has won, it plans not merely to redraw the map of the world; it plans, also, a new order in which new principles of governance will control men's lives. The decision that Great Britain has to make is either—and at almost any cost—to break the power of Hitler and his allies or to surrender, for any period that it is necessary for this generation to consider, her major place among the nations of the world.

What, at long last, Great Britain has come to see is that it is for her citizens a question now of victory or of annihilation; there is no middle term between the two. To appease Hitler, clearly enough, is no longer a possible task. That effort was made over six grim and mistaken years; its only result was to increase his power and enlarge his ambitions. No peace with him could be an enduring peace unless it was one that he imposed, for no peace satisfies him save that in which the other party to the treaty is wholly within his hands. If, as at Munich, he temporizes, it is only to crouch for a new spring. He knows no objective worthy of consideration except power for the sake of power. Justice, generosity, mercy, freedom, none of these has meaning for him as he goes forward. He denies rights to any nationality which will not accept subordination to him. He looks with contempt upon the claims of the common people of every country, even, indeed, of his own. He does not regard his pledged word as more than a counter in the unceasing game of power. It is the immanent logic at once of his methods and of his purpose that he must destroy or be destroyed.

For the social order he would create, were he to be successful, is one that we now fully understand.

To many, even to many Englishmen, it was, until only the other day, no more than a madman's dream. They could not bring themselves to believe that any child of the twentieth century could seriously contemplate a world in which the vast majority were the helpless slaves of a cruel and corrupt oligarchy, ruling by the right of force alone, and concerned deliberately to emphasize their conviction that force alone is a full title to rule. They could not bring themselves, either, to believe that a group of outlaws—for that, in essence, is what the Nazi leaders are—could not only secure the hold of the state-power of a great people, but could also mould the habits of that people in service to the ways of outlawry. They knew that power was in its nature hard. They were convinced that when the outlaws had hacked their way to its confident possession they would develop that sense of responsibility suited to the conditions which peace in the twentieth century of the Christian Era requires. They recognized that part, at least, of the outlaws' rise to power was the result of defeat inflicted upon Germany and of the wrongs and suffering always associated with defeat. They assumed that when the wrongs had been righted and the sufferings assuaged all would be well. They even searched in the *mores* of the new Germany—as in the previous decade they had searched in the *mores* of the new Italy—for principles of social behaviour that they could utilize

[14]

for their own peoples with advantage. Their diplomacy assumed that Hitler and his colleagues were, on the whole men rather like themselves—ambitious, no doubt, strained by the experiences through which they had passed but capable of adjusting themselves to the historic framework of European order. It did not occur to them until it was too late that their view was wholly mistaken.

They were not dealing, as it is vital to understand, with revolutionaries who made war, whether social or international, upon the principles of a doctrine susceptible of rational examination. Argument with Hitler was sterile, since, as an outlaw, he was the very symbol of irrationality. The principles by which they lived meant nothing to him because those principles were in fact the framework of that social order which symbolized his defeat. He had come to power by their defiance and their destruction; he could maintain himself in power only by continuing to defy and to destroy them. If, in the international sphere, he temporized with them for six years, that was only that he might the better prepare himself for their overthrow. They wanted peace and security; as an outlaw, he understood that exactly these were fatal to his power. The outlaw cannot observe the rules and continue as outlaw, for it is the essence of the rules that they set limit to the outlaw's power. He might hold them off with protestations and insistences that he sought only to repair this wrong or to mitigate that injustice; at every point that, as they were driven to see, was only the cunning of the outlaw who evades the law while he prepares for attack. Hitler was not a revolutionary in the sense that Luther or Calvin, Marx or Lenin, was a revolutionary; he did not aim, even in the service of his ambition, at an end beyond himself which sought the transvaluation of all values. He was simply and entirely an outlaw to whom all values were devoid of meaning. It was above all by the methods of the outlaw that he had attained power, and he knew no other methods by which to retain it.

It took, as I have said, more than six years for the rulers of Europe to begin to awaken to the realization that this was true; it took more than eight months of war before the lesson of the awakening dawned upon them. When it did, almost all Europe was prostrate at Hitler's feet, and nothing except the power of Great Britain stood in the way of his full triumph. That position has been compared with the similar situation of lonely eminence which Great Britain occupied in 1806. Then, as now, she defied the conqueror of a prostrate Europe and emerged, after a long struggle, victorious from the ordeal. By holding out, by maintaining successfully her dominion upon the seas, she was able to take advantage of the rising tide of national feeling which, first in Spain and then in Germany, found the yoke of tyranny unendurable. At the end, Great Britain found herself presiding over a vast coalition of those who had suffered from the agonies of Napoleonic despotism. Few could have thought that the proud conqueror of Austerlitz and Jena would, in so brief a time, set out on the lonely journey to the barren exile of St. Helena. Yet the miracle happened. And, granted resolution of a similar quality today, the miracle can happen again. The British people knows what is in store for it if it is defeated. That knowledge will steel it yet again to the endurance which offers the promise of victory.

So runs the argument of the British rulers. And I think it is a valid argument upon certain conditions. It is valid if we learn to understand why the first nine months of war have been a grim period of bitter defeat. It is valid, also, if we are prepared to recognize the sacrifices victory will entail and to pay the price it will exact. Analogies with the past are important, but they are not decisive. It is mere rhetoric to say that we shall win because we are free men battling against slaves. It is mere rhetoric, also, to say that we shall win because we fight the battle of civilization against an evil barbarism. Free men have been beaten before by the legions of slavery; and, were we to lose, it would not be the first time that the barbarians have conquered civilization.

It is, I think, profoundly true that Great Britain

[17]

is now the last refuge of civilization in Europe; and
it is also not less profoundly true that upon its power
to hold depends the recovery of European freedom.
But we have to realize two things if we are to
recognize the strength of the enemy we confront.
Nazism, and its satellite Mussolini, are in a position
which makes their hope of victory at least a legitimate gamble because the rulers of the main European states acquiesced in their rise to, and
consolidation of, power. Unless we draw the right
inferences from this fact, we shall not assess the
significance of those with whom we are in conflict.
And, secondly, we must realize that in each of the
states Nazism has been able to overthrow, part, at
least, of its will to resistance was overthrown before
the actual warfare began. Here, again, an understanding of why this should have been so is a
fundamental condition of victory. It is not enough
to know that there are traitors within the gate;
it is still more important to know both why they
are there and how we can remedy the conditions
that make them ready to co-operate in betrayal.

The war, in a word, has not come because two
evil and ambitious men seized power in two great
European states and determined to extend their
power by war. Hitler and Mussolini are the outcome of profound historical forces which are not
of today or yesterday. The causes which have led

[18]

to their victories are not a series of unfortunate accidents but deep-rooted in our society. The Battle of France was not lost because Weygand replaced Gamelin when it was already too late. The pitiful surrender of France was not consummated merely because a handful of corrupt politicians exploited the once-heroic name of a pitiful old man in their haste to save what they could from the wreckage. "If I am told," wrote Montesquieu, "that a great nation has been lost through the fortune of a single battle, I do not believe it; I search for the general causes which led it to lose the battle."

So, too, with the defeat of Poland, and the over-running of Scandinavia and the Low Countries. Poland was not defeated in a fortnight; her over-throw was the consummation of twenty-one years of outmoded and corrupt oligarchy. The overrun-ning of Scandinavia and the Low Countries can be attributed to their tragic faith in an obsolete system of neutrality; but that still leaves unexplained why, despite its obvious obsolescence, they still clung so pathetically to their faith in its validity.

More than this: the vast majority of us are agreed today that Hitler and Mussolini are evil men. But it would be easy to compile a long list of notable Englishmen who, as it were but yesterday, were eagerly applauding their achievements and jostling one another in their anxiety to lay wreaths upon

[19]

their altars. Yet nothing in either's nature has changed; the only difference is that the ambit of their malevolence now includes our own fortunes, whereas, until the other day, we hoped that it might be turned in another direction. We have to understand what it is that made some of our leaders enthusiastic about the men they now condemn, when those men are only fulfilling a programme no item of which was ever concealed and about each item of which they were consistently warned.

Politics, in short, is unintelligible if we simplify it to the point of making it the struggle of right against wrong, of good men against evil. It is unintelligible, also, unless we see it in its historical perspective; otherwise it becomes immune to rational analysis and is a tale devoid of meaning. I think myself that we are fighting what Mr. Chamberlain called "the evil things," and I think, also, that we have still the power and the will to overthrow them. But I think it is immensely important that Mr. Chamberlain, whom I use only as the symbol of a large number of spectators, refused to admit that they were "evil things" until Hitler and Mussolini demanded the surrender of interests it would have been impossible for him to yield. That blindness, half excusable, half deliberate, enabled Mr. Chamberlain to persuade himself to accept as victories, in Abyssinia and Austria, in Spain and

[20]

Czechoslovakia, what we now all recognize to have
been immense defeats. It enabled him for six grim
years to be deaf to the cries of these victims of
Nazi tyranny whose sufferings he suddenly discovered as a proof of intolerable barbarism after
the declaration of war. It is to the foundations which
underlie these attitudes that we must go if we are
to appreciate in a serious way the situation we oc-
cupy. Only in the knowledge of our circumstances
is there the possibility of a programme for victory.

II

What we are witnessing is the breakdown of a
social order which, broadly speaking, has dominated
Europe since the French Revolution. It is a social
order in which the effective economic power has,
again broadly speaking, been in the hands of the
middle and upper classes who have used the power
of the state to safeguard the privileges inherent in
their possession of economic power. But, as the
French Revolution made clear, the middle class alone
was not powerful enough to overthrow that feudal
aristocracy which previously possessed the authority of the state. To do so, it had to invoke the aid of
the masses, and that involved the development of
capitalist democracy. It was a social order in which,
increasingly as the nineteenth century developed,
formal political power remained with the masses

while the substantial authority of the state remained
with the owners of property. It has been the essential feature of capitalist democracy throughout
its history that, while it conferred material concessions of great importance upon the workers, it
still left them dependent upon the owners of property for the effective right to live by the sale of
their labour-power.

For the motive to production was profit; without
profit there was no employment to be had. To
jeopardize the ability to make profit was, therefore,
to jeopardize the opportunity of the workers to sell
their labour-power. The history of the past hundred
and fifty years is largely the history of the effort
of the workers to humanize the conditions under
which they sold that labour-power. It is a history
which operates on two interdependent planes—
that of economic organization and that of political
organization. It is the history, also, of the immense
growth of the power to produce, and of capital accumulation. But because the power to produce must
mean, by the logic of the system, the ability to sell
at a profit, and because, by the same logic, the
incentive to accumulate depends also upon the ability to invest profitably, the drive of capitalism is
always to the widest possible market in which the
highest possible profit can be found. Competition
is always driving profits to a minimum, and, in the

absence of countervailing frictions, the standards
of labour also. And this makes the relation of capitalism and democracy always an unstable one.

For it is the inherent tendency of all capital to
get the highest profit it can, and its owners develop
a way of life from their experience which they seek
to protect with all the weapons the law places at
their disposal. But it is the inherent tendency of
democracy to produce in the masses an urge to use
their political power for material economic benefits
not otherwise available to them. So long as the working of the system gives them full employment at a
steadily rising standard of life, they tend to be content with its operations. But as soon as economic
difficulties develop, they seek to use their political
power to mitigate the effects of those difficulties
upon their lives.

I cannot stay, at this point, to discuss how the
result of this contradiction between the economic
and the political nature of the state transformed
it into the social-service state we know; nor can I
seek to trace the development of that finance-capital,
correlated with political imperialism, by which the
owning classes in the major states have sought to
pay the costs of the social services they were compelled to establish while they strove, at the same
time, to maintain the privileges of ownership to
which they had grown accustomed. The vital point

[23]

is that, by the beginning of the twentieth century, a situation had developed in which rival imperialisms were competing with one another for the power to exploit the major sources of profit. Upon their ability to obtain that power depended their chance of maintaining the uneasy equilibrium between capitalism and democracy. Without it, they would find themselves compelled fundamentally to reorganize the foundations of their economic systems.

Here lies the root of the conflict of 1914. It was, in essence, a struggle for markets between the rising power of Germany and allied empires threatened by German economic ambitions. The economic systems of the combatants were conditioned to that form of national state which had arisen out of the collapse of feudalism, and they encountered the difficulty that their political expressions were incompatible with their economic needs. It is no doubt true that a score of minor motivations combined to give complexity to the struggle. The feeling of national solidarity, dynastic ambition, the fear of socialism, the sense that union against a foe without postpones the need to heal internal rivalries of classes, the sentiment, as between Russian and Serb, of racial affinity, all played their part in the struggle. But essentially it was a conflict of rival imperialisms to obtain the control of the major unexploited sources of profitable enterprise.

Where We Stand Today

The background of the peace which ended the war of 1914 is marked, above all, I think, by three features. The first is the Russian Revolution. An old and evil tyranny collapsed under the pressure of defeat, and it was replaced by a system which put a new economic class in possession of the state. That revolution, like its predecessor of 1789, was an explicit threat to the existing social order. It aroused the same hates and the same hopes. It exacerbated the internal conflicts in every state because, on the one hand, it aroused the fear of insecurity among the possessing classes, while, on the other, it stimulated the workers to the sense that they could in justice, as they thought, claim far better conditions than had ever been conceded to them. The Russian Revolution, in a word, brought to a head that conflict over the place of property in society which had been a matter of fierce debate ever since the development of the factory system had made possible effective trade unionism, and the members of the trade unions had, in the main, linked their political fortunes to Socialist doctrine.

The second feature of the peace was its transformation of Germany into a capitalist democracy with a responsible system of government simultaneously with military defeat and national humiliation. That meant a Germany riddled with contradictions its leaders did not know how to solve. The democracy

[25]

wanted large concessions in the social sphere; economic distress made these impossible within the framework of capitalism. The owners of property wanted security and the ability to recover the prospect of profit; these they could win not under the shadow of a price exacted by defeat and the general economic misery. The failure of the government adequately to satisfy any class deprived it of the authority to govern with determination. The presence of a great army of unemployed, the destruction of middle-class savings in the inflation of 1923, the insult of the invasion of the Ruhr, all combined to deprive the democratic system of any deep roots in the affection of the German people. Democracy there was born in humiliation and nourished in failure. It won contempt from Communists, who saw in it only an experiment that had lacked the courage to go forward to social revolution. It earned the hatred of business enterprise, which could not discover within its framework the conditions of economic recovery. It was naturally loathed by the old Junker class, to whose still-remaining power it was a permanent threat; and it never won the allegiance of the army and the ex-officer class, to whom it was the symbol of their defeat. It hardly secured, even, the loyalty of the main body of its civil servants, whose minds and habits were shaped to the traditions of the previous regimes. It could not win the affection of the younger generation, to which its psychological and economic conditions represented above all the frustration of opportunity. And since the political traditions a democracy requires were still new in post-war Germany, they could hardly take root in a soil unfavourable to the growth of that agreement upon fundamentals in doctrine which is the condition of success in democratic government.

The third feature of the peace, I think, was that it came upon a world habituated by four years of war to the practice of violence and never sufficiently at one with itself to recover from that practice. For that recovery depended upon the ability of men to feel that they had a real and continuous chance of improving their life-condition. They were massively deprived of that opportunity. Mainly they were deprived of it by economic crisis and the social and political conditions which flowed from that crisis. Vast unemployment; increasing restrictions upon free migration above all to the New World; the development of every sort of device to prevent the free flow of foreign trade at the expense of the domestic producer; the growth of taxation to meet both the cost of maintaining the unemployed and the satisfaction of the new level of workers' demands released by the psychological pressure of the war— these are some of the main causes why the violence

of the war remained a natural part of men's behaviour in the peace. They wanted a settled and
secure world. They found themselves in one which
seemed incapable of either. And the deeper the disturbance in economic conditions, the deeper, in
parallel succession, was the psychological inability
to find the terms of unity.

I am not arguing for one moment that the peace
made in 1919 was fundamentally an unjust peace.
Some of its features were bad; the method of its
negotiation was unpardonable. But it is, I think,
true to say that, in the face of incredibly difficult
conditions, the statesmen who made it left a Europe
more justly organized than the one they had found.
They even sought to build, in the League of Nations, an instrument of world peace which would
correct the errors that they had made. But that instrument was defective for two vital reasons. Since,
first, it preserved the principle of state sovereignty,
it meant that the interests of the whole were always
at the mercy of any vested interest which viewed
policy in the light of its own selfish concerns; the
League was a policy-making, not a law-making body.
It reflected that disproportion between the world
market and the national state which was one of the
half-dozen fundamental facts of the post-war world.
And it could never transcend that disproportion,
because the economic environment in which the

principle of state sovereignty compelled it to function was never beneficent enough to persuade its more powerful members to the sacrifices needed for the correction of that disproportion. To keep the peace, the League would have needed to be either much less or much more than it was. As much less, it might have kept the peace as a tight alliance of the victors determined to keep down defeated states like Germany or disappointed states like Italy; but the victors did not retain enough of a common purpose to make that possible. As much more, it might have kept the peace by developing into an organization with a genuine power to legislate for the common interest of its members. But to have done so those members would have had to be persuaded to abrogate their sovereignty, and this none, at least of the major states, could afford to do without solving the central contradiction within itself between capitalism and democracy.

For it is to that central contradiction that the problem always goes back. Their relationship is satisfactory in periods of economic expansion; it becomes difficult in periods of economic contraction. To maintain the procedures of democracy when these seem to threaten objectives to which an important group in the society attaches a fundamental importance is always hard, for history makes it only too clear that men's approval of means can never be dissociated from the ends to which those means are devoted. Capitalist democracy was a compromise in general approved by capitalists so long as its democratic aspect did not threaten the foundations of capitalism. But when that threat was judged to be real, and when, because it was so judged, the owners felt that their privileges were in danger, their enthusiasm for democracy suffered a notable diminution, and their power to abridge its authority was sharpened by two facts. The first was that the perspective of all their thinking was shaped by a culture all the implications of which assumed their right to power. Economic doctrine was a metaphysic which rationalized their means. The classic political philosophy assumed the neutrality of the state and obscured the reality that its laws were intended to protect their right to its continuance. Their educational system for the most part was a schooling of the masses in the right of the successful to power; nothing shows that better than the substance of historical teaching. Their jurisprudence prided itself upon accepting the principle of equality before the law; it rarely emphasized the fact that men are equal before the law only when they have the financial means to take advantage of its procedures.

The growth of working-class organizations, in every society based upon universal suffrage and

democratic procedures, was a challenge to this culture, a challenge, after 1917, made ever more explicit by the impact of the Russian Revolution. It
revived all the fears of democracy which had been
so eloquently expressed by middle-class thinkers
at the time of the revolutions of 1848, by Macaulay,
by de Tocqueville, a little later by Walter Bagehot.
The question came into the foreground whether
democracy based on universal suffrage was compati-
ble with the regime of private property. It began
to be pointed out that the price of social legislation
was more than the system could afford. Some considered that too many people were being educated
beyond their station; they were even beginning, said
an eminent churchman, to compete with the children of the middle class for the best positions in the
state. A leading Conservative politician could write
that too many people concerned themselves with
politics; that was an occupation for the few, and
the many should devote themselves to religious
faith in which can be found consolations for the
inadequacies of this world. There were suggestions
that the unemployed in receipt of relief might prop-
erly be disfranchised—an obvious return to the Eliza-
bethan sense of the danger of the "sturdy vagabond."
What is certain is that in the period after 1919
the sense that property was in danger from democracy was omnipresent in Europe and, after 1929, in

the United States also. The working of the economic system did not satisfy the masses, and there was the profound fear that the masses might use democratic institutions to transform the economic system.

The second fact was the discovery that the weapons in the hands of the owners of property were far more formidable than they imagined. If progressive governments attained power, they had only to withdraw their confidence and the authority of such governments was rapidly impaired. That was true of Britain in 1924 and 1931; it was true of France in 1924, 1924, 1932, and 1936. It was true of the Roosevelt administration in the United States; Mr. Roosevelt had either to sacrifice, or to whittle down, his major experiments in order to secure the cooperation of the owners of economic power. And if, as in Austria and Italy, in Spain and Germany, the masses did not show signs of accepting the permanent title of those owners to their privileges, these owners took the direct step to their preservation by suppressing the democratic institutions which seemed to threaten them.

It is important, moreover, to remember that in all the capitalist democracies the vital positions of control were effectively barred from access to the masses. In Great Britain, for example, the officers of the defence services, the higher civil service, the judicial bench, even the professoriate of the universities, were overwhelmingly staffed from the middle and upper classes. They owned, too, the organs of public opinion. They dominated the direction of the banks and insurance companies and of the great corporations. They filled all the great proconsular and diplomatic posts. "It cannot be right," wrote Lord Acton, "that one party should have retained the making of the laws, the management of the conditions, the keeping of the peace, the administration of justice, the distribution of taxes, the control of expenditure, in its own hands exclusively." Yet that was the situation inherent in the nature of capitalist democracy.

It was a situation, in short, in which there was no economic security for most citizens, no real equality of opportunity—even conservative observers have drawn attention to the increasing class-stratification of the United States—in which, also, the ability to realize many of the main possibilities of liberty were dependent upon the possession of property. If it was true that the power of the aristocracy had been broken, there was a fundamental sense in which that power had been replaced by the power of a plutocracy; and it was, as de Tocqueville had foreseen a century ago, at least doubtful whether the change was of social advantage. For the social responsibility of an aristocracy at its best is profounder than that of a plutocracy which works always within limits set narrowly by that profit-making motive upon which it depends. Its habit is, as it were, to see social organization as if it were a company balance-sheet and to argue that human needs must conform to the requirements and standards of the business man. Its tendency was to assume that where democratic institutions interfered with those requirements and those standards, their validity was, at the best, doubtful.

Now the working of democratic institutions depends, in any society, upon what Lord Balfour called an agreement upon fundamentals; it has still to be demonstrated that they will operate successfully when men are deeply divided about matters of ultimate social constitution. It was into such a period that men passed in the years after 1919. The division is shown in many ways. It was exhibited in the attitude to the results of the Russian Revolution. It was exhibited in the attitude to Fascism in Italy. It was exhibited in the attitude of the owning class to the General Strike of 1926 in Britain, to the New Deal in America, to the Popular Front Government in France. It is significant, above all, in this period that liberal parties tended to yield their hold upon the allegiance of the working class to Socialist and, on the Continent, to Communist Parties; and even if the vote for the last of these is regarded less as a definitive allegiance to a doctrine than as the protest of despair at suffering,

[34]

it is still significant, first, because it revealed a mental climate among the workers which rejected the claims of capitalism to any further confidence, and, second, because the eclipse of liberalism obviously had the result of setting the owners of economic power on their guard against democratic institutions. The position was increasingly realized of which Bagehot had spoken in 1867, when he urged the propertied classes to form an alliance to resist the pressure of democracy.

I am arguing, in fact, that the lesson of the post-war years was a simple one. It was the lesson that the acceptance of democracy by capitalism was conditioned by the always-implicit understanding that the concessions demanded by the former must not go beyond the limits deemed reasonable by the latter. I am arguing, further, that capitalism's conception of what was reasonable was limited by two factors—the economic crisis on the one hand, and the profound fears engendered by the Russian Revolution on the other. The psychological effects of these were momentous. They meant, all over the world, a panic-stricken search by property for security; and many of the measures it took in the interests of security—the restrictionist measures, for instance, because they had the effect of only deepening the economic crisis—still further enhanced the sense of insecurity.

Where Do We Go from Here?

When men feel insecure, they grow afraid; and
the mood of fear is unfavourable to the use of reason. But democratic institutions depend for their
hold upon the power of reason over men's minds.
Their purpose is to make possible a procedure of
consent instead of a procedure of coercion; but a
procedure of consent argues that men can see that
one argument is better than another. It was this atmosphere that was increasingly absent after 1919.
That is why, everywhere, the traditional values
broke down. That is why the same event could seem
so utterly different to men differently placed. The
General Strike of 1926, for example, seemed to millions of trade unionists a simple demonstration
of solidarity for the miners' standard of life; to the
main part of the middle and upper classes in Great
Britain it seemed a revolutionary assault upon the
Constitution. To Lord Lloyd and others like him,
Mussolini even as late as the winter of 1939 seemed
the man who had restored working-class discipline
in Italy while safeguarding all the due rights of
Italian labour; to the normal trade unionist in Great
Britain, Mussolini was the *condottiere* of Italian big
business who had destroyed democracy and the
defence-mechanisms of the workers in the interests
of Italian big business. When Mr. Ramsay Mac-
Donald formed his National Government in 1931,

[36]

he seemed to the Labour Party to have betrayed every principle he had ever preached; to the middle and upper classes of Great Britain he was the architect of national salvation. By 1936 Mr. Roosevelt was as deeply loved by the workers of the United States as he was hated by its financial interests. The working class of France gave M. Léon Blum the position of the first Socialist Prime Minister of France and, significantly enough, the last of the Third Republic, at the same time as M. Charles Maurras, not without applause from the Right, was calling for his assassination.

It is needless to multiply instances. The point I want to make is that circumstances made men look so differently, within each national society, upon the working of democratic institutions that they seemed no longer to speak the same language. And if that difference is related to the total circumstances of the time, it is difficult not to feel that all the main factors were present which portend social convulsion. Wide disparities of wealth and power, between nations no less than between classes, are deeply resented. The disinherited make those signs of protest which issue in conflict, and the protest, even in the most liberal countries, has encountered angry repression. There has been a temper of hostility to free discussion which has everywhere reached grave proportions. Not since 1848 has the settlement of social differences so easily issued in violence.

And it is significant that this social and political *malaise* has been accompanied by a challenge to contemporary standards of culture more profound than any since the birth of the Romantic movement —itself the portent of a challenge to a given way of life. There has been a decay of all the values upon which our civilization has been built, a decline in the power of tradition to hold the allegiance of men. Some, in despair, have sought to escape into a defence of individualism, or by recommending esoteric Oriental philosophies which have no serious relation to the conditions we confront. The decline of the traditional religious faiths into a polite ceremonial expressing a creed upon which most people do not dream of acting has been remarkable. The governing class has lost confidence in itself; that is the only possible explanation of the absence of a power to lead in an epoch in which, above all, direction was required. The main body of our literature, like that of the eighteenth century in France, is almost wholly, in its serious manifestation, one of criticism and dissent; and if it be said that there are few men of letters with a positive faith to offer, that does not lessen the importance of the fact that their emphasis is essentially negation.

The post-war years have been feverish and frustrated years; the absence both of security and of self-confidence is not the less notable even when it disguises itself under the name of realism. That sense of frustration is significantly evident among the scientists and technologists who declare that their power to lessen the burden of mankind is thwarted by the economic and social institutions of our time. Not less important is the rising of the subject peoples, above all in the Far East, but, significantly enough, in Africa also. Having accepted for more than a century the domination of Western civilization, they see in its apparent disintegration not only the chance of their own liberation, but also the lesson that they had an art of life which the West destroyed.

We seem, in fact, to have reached a point in social evolution where we have discovered the secret of efficiency, but have no great end to which to devote it. We have never had riches so great within our grasp; we have never been so insecure as we seek them. Our level of education is higher than in any other age, yet its main result has been the intensification of our discontents. We have become, economically, an interdependent world; we cannot break those vested interests which prevent our building the institutions that would express that interdependence. The result is the tragic one that, while the peoples of the world are hungry for security and peace, the only prospect we can offer them is a bleak horizon of insecurity and war. The civilization, in fact, that was built upon the ruins of medieval Christendom is ending in division and disillusion. It has lost any united consciousness of a faith which binds it together. Private interest triumphs over the common interest, and it uses the state-power in the reckless effort to preserve its privileges. The traditional wisdom of bourgeois society has broken down because its operation no longer shelters the masses from the blasts of life in the conditions they deem adequate to their claims. And because men think differently who live differently, the rulers of that society cannot admit the validity of those claims, since response to them would involve the sacrifice of those privileges and that prestige which time has taught them to regard as rights. In the result, men have ceased to be able to reason together. Fearful of the morrow, they denounce one another, and what were yesterday rights admitted and claims considered, today are held to be crimes. Here it is a crime to be a rich man, there a crime to be a trade unionist. We have moved to an age of new creed wars as real, and not less

[40]

ferocious, than those of the Reformation; wars, be
it noted, in which men's consciences are not less
deeply engaged. I do not think it is mistaken to
regard these signs as an index to the end of an
age.

III

The characteristics of which I have spoken emerge
most clearly if we consider briefly the foreign policies
which immediately preceded the war, and the actual
conduct of the democracies in conflict up to the
capitulation of France. In considering them, I make
one assumption only—that the democracies confronted two aggressive tyrannies which were driven
by their inherent nature to conquests and that these
could be achieved only at the expense of the democracies. The problems we have to consider are, first,
why the democracies did not act against the tyrannies until the latter had been given immense victories and the fullest opportunity to prepare; and,
second, why the tyrannies, after hostilities began,
were able—up to the capitulation of France—to
break so easily their antagonists' will to resistance.

Part, at any rate, of that inability to act is due
to the hatred of the democracies for war, and there
is a real truth in the assertion that when their leaders, as over Czechoslovakia, acquiesced in aggression
which they could not defend, they were expressing

the sentiments of no inconsiderable part of the opinion upon which they depended for their authority. No one, I think, who is aware of either the nature of modern war or the grim responsibilities which decisions to embark upon it must cast on the statesmen who have to take them can fail to understand why they should have shrunk from those responsibilities.

But when that is said, much still remains to be said. No democratic statesman now doubts that the regimes of Hitler and Mussolini are a threat to everything worth preserving in our civilization. But all that they threaten today they have threatened continuously since their seizure of power; all that has happened since September 3, 1939, is their opportunity to exercise their tyranny over an immensely wider theatre. In the years after 1933 the democracies had painful evidence that the dictators had limitless ambitions and were deaf to all considerations of pity and honour and fair play. They heard the cries of their victims; they even ventured some timid protests at the victimization. They were warned by the working-class movements of the whole world that the outcome of the policy inaugurated by the dictators was, inevitably, war. They were urged to organize collective security against aggression; even economic sanctions, Mr. Chamberlain declared, "were midsummer madness." They let Austria and

[42]

Spain and Czechoslovakia be immolated in grim succession upon the altar of the dictators' appetites. They refused, until the eleventh hour, to discuss with the Soviet Union the possibility of joint action against aggression. Having refused to protect from disaster the democracies of Spain and Czechoslovakia, when they saw that no "appeasement" could satisfy the dictators, they were profuse in guarantees of protection to semi-Fascist states like Poland and Greece and Rumania, even though, in the absence of an agreement with the Soviet Union, the folly of these guarantees was obvious. Nor did they, in the period when the drift of war was deemed unmistakable, embark upon preparations in any degree commensurate with the dangers they confronted.

What is the explanation of this attitude? The answer, I am confident, lies in that contradiction between capitalism and democracy of which I have spoken. In the period before the outbreak of war, Hitler and Mussolini commended themselves to the forces of privilege in the democracies for two reasons. In the first place, they had disciplined working-class institutions and thereby had rescued the forces of privilege from the insecurity that these implied. In the second place, they represented themselves as the fervent opponents of Bolshevism. From this, two implications were drawn. The first was that,

should either Hitler or Mussolini be overthrown,
Bolshevism would be the residuary legatee of his
overthrow; to keep them in power, therefore, was
to hold back the spread of the major doctrine
inimical to privilege. This it is, for example, which
can alone explain the extraordinary tenderness displayed by the Bank of England to Hitler, and by
American financial interests to Mussolini, during
the consolidation of their power; the attitude of Mr.
Montagu Norman to the Czech deposits in the Bank
for International Settlements will always remain a
shameful item in our diplomatic history. The second
implication was the belief, drawn from a pathetic
acceptance of the dictators' avowals at their face
value, that skilful appeasement of their ambitions in
Western Europe would lead them, especially Hitler,
to seek for an extension of their power at the expense of the Soviet Union. Hitler might be led into
an attempt to be the executioner of Bolshevism. If
he succeeded, the main menace to privilege would
be removed without cost to Britain and France, and
the process would sufficiently exhaust him to safeguard them from any menace he would then present. If he failed, an end would be put to his
aggressive system without direct cost to the capitalist
democracies; and they had good reason to believe
that the Soviet Union had no dreams of imperialist
expansion at their expense. That, of course, is why

the effort to come to an understanding with the Soviet Union was so long postponed.

The great powers among the democracies were, this is to say, at no point free from a very real sympathy with the dictators, not least because their privileged classes sympathized with some of the results of their rule. That came out with startling clarity in the Spanish Civil War, when those classes were loud in their enthusiasm for the rebels against the constitutional government, and when the governments of Great Britain and France did not hesitate to refuse to the Republicans that right to purchase arms which was theirs by international law, and deliberately chose to close their eyes to the fact that the rebels' victory was being organized for them by Germany and Italy. They were even prepared to close their eyes to the strategic consequences to both of them of the reduction of Spain to the position of a client-state of the dictators. They never even considered the importance to them, in the event of a war with the dictators, of a friendly and democratic Spain. And they compelled the surrender of Czechoslovakia, not only in disregard of solemn engagements, but with a purblind resolve not to assess the immense addition to Hitler's strength which its betrayal involved. It is difficult not to feel, as we survey the history of these years, that there was no surrender the major capitalist democracies

[45]

would not have made to the dictators so long as they could have the assurance that they would not interfere with their own vested interests and would seek their compensation elsewhere.

For it seems, indeed, true to say that the rulers of Great Britain and France had to be driven by an outraged public opinion into action against the dictators, and the way in which they shunned the prospect of any association with the Soviet Union, the way, further, in which, having been driven to attempt that collaboration by public opinion, they shuffled and evaded realism in negotiation, show clearly that for them the real enemy was not in Berlin or Rome but in Moscow. They were playing the historic game of power-politics without using the main trump-card—Germany's fear of a war on two fronts—that was in their hands. Their policy convinced, quite intelligibly, the Soviet Union that their main purpose was to use it as the main theatre of German attack. The Soviet Union had for years been treated like a pariah, and the character of the negotiations convinced its leaders that neither Great Britain nor France was sincere in its search for a defensive pact. They understood, too, that the guarantee to Poland was, in fact, a guarantee of the western frontiers of the Soviet Union, and one which, as it were, had been given to them without charge; for once it had been given, if Germany at-

tacked Poland, France and Great Britain would
have no alternative but to make war upon her.
Granted the German desire to avoid a major war on
two fronts, this gave the Soviet Union not only the
chance to assure its own neutrality, but to exact
a price for it which went, at any rate, a considerable
distance toward guaranteeing its frontiers against
German aggression. Having thus secured all that
it could ask from Germany, the Soviet Union had
no further interest in negotiations with France and
Great Britain. These found themselves with that
war upon their hands which it should have been their
supreme effort to avoid.

I myself think that, on a long-term view, the
Soviet policy was a mistaken one. It not only enormously increased the chances of success for powers
which, if victorious, were certain sooner or later
to have their reckoning with Moscow; it had the
two further consequences of going far, by its cynical
implication, to destroy the hold the Soviet Union
possessed on the allegiance of the working class all
over the world, and it thus precipitated the possibility that, at some future stage, without interference from the workers, capitalism, whether in
its democratic or in its dictatorial form, would
make that attack on Bolshevism it had been the con-
sistent purpose of Soviet diplomacy to avoid. The
revelation that Stalin would play power-politics as

cynically as did Mr. Chamberlain or M. Bonnet destroyed a faith in the Soviet Union which, as the action of the British workers in 1920 had shown, was a bulwark of strength to it. Coupled with the attack on Finland, in which it displayed all the worst features of Machiavellian statecraft, it left its supporters all over the world in a position in which they could legitimately be accused of having precipitated the war and of being guilty of exactly the same kind of aggression as that of which they had been the main accusers when the aggressors had been the Fascist powers. And they left the "appeasers" with the power to assert that they had always known that no reliance could be placed upon the Soviet Union.

The breakdown of the plans for a common front with the Soviet Union against the Fascist powers still lies essentially at the door of Great Britain and France. It was the outcome of a twenty years' relation of hostility and cold neglect, built upon the hope of its breakdown before 1933 and of German attack upon it after that period; and the three months' frenzied effort at a bargain in which the negotiators seemed deliberately to be chosen to contrast the importance attached to "appeasement" of Germany with the contempt felt for the Soviet Union goes far to explain, even while it does not wholly excuse, Moscow's refusal to believe in the sincerity of the

Franco-British offer. Indeed, so far as the British and French governments were concerned, it is difficult to believe in their sincerity. Sir Nevile Henderson's account of his final days in Berlin shows clearly that, if he interpreted rightly the attitude of the British government, it would have been quite willing to "appease" Hitler again if the manner of his demands upon Poland had not been of so threatening a character. They embarked upon war because the bulk of public opinion in each country would not have permitted them to make another Munich. That public opinion, above all among the workers, saw clearly two things which neither of the governments wanted to see. It saw clearly, first, that further "appeasement" would put Germany in a position of such overwhelming strength that the democracies would hardly be able to resist its claims at a later stage; and it saw, second, not less clearly, that this strength would give the governments of Britain and France an equally overwhelming interest in pushing Germany to be the executioner of the Soviet experiment. Both Mr. Chamberlain and M. Daladier might declare that they had striven with all their might to avoid war, but it could be not less truly said of both of them that in their efforts they had deliberately avoided the one policy which could have made it successful.

And this emerges most clearly in the attitude of

[49]

the smaller European powers. All of them feared
Germany; all of them knew that a German victory
meant an end of their independence. Yet all of them
declared a neutrality that none of them was in a
position to defend from German attack, because
all of them had ceased to place any reliance upon
the will, perhaps even the power, of the greater
democracies to protect them. That was the inference
they had drawn from the policy pursued since the
occupation of Manchuria by Japan in 1931. They
had seen the greater democracies flout the Covenant
of the League. They had watched the half-hearted
attempt, in the background of the dishonourable
Hoare-Laval Treaty, to apply sanctions to Italy. They
had noted that first Czechoslovakia and then Spain
were sacrificed to Hitler and Mussolini; that in the
first case the statesmen of the greater democracies
boasted of their achievement in securing the sacrifice without conflict, and that in the second the Foreign Secretary of Great Britain could say of the
struggle of a people to emancipate itself that the
issue was "a faction fight in which we are not interested." However mistaken, it was natural enough
for the smaller democracies to cling to an outworn
concept of neutrality, in the faint hope that by some
miracle the tempest of war would pass them by. That
pathetic effort to remain neutral is the supreme measure of condemnation for the policy pursued by the

governments of Great Britain and France. It was essentially an announcement that, whatever their fears of Germany, they had no real faith in the bona fides of the anti-Fascist powers.

Only collective security could have saved Europe from war; the British and French governments consciously wrecked collective security, and they therefore got their war. They wrecked collective security because to have organized it seriously would have meant an alliance with the Soviet Union, on the one hand, and the downfall of Hitler and Mussolini on the other. They feared the first because they saw in its ideas a threat to the vested interests they represented, and they feared the second because they saw in it implications of social revolution they were not prepared to confront. They were ready to maintain Hitler and Mussolini in power—nothing else explains either the statements of Sir Nevile Henderson or Mr. Chamberlain's praise of Mussolini in the very speech in which he declared war on the major partner in the Axis—so long as they did not threaten interests which Great Britain and France regarded as fundamental. To avoid that threat, as the examples of Spain and Czechoslovakia showed, they were prepared for immense sacrifices at the expense of other peoples. It was only when their peoples, rather than the governments of France and Britain, made it evident that they would not parley

[51]

further with aggression that Mr. Chamberlain and
M. Daladier issued their challenge.

I see no alternative inference in the experience
of these years but that, on balance, the capitalist
democracies hoped against hope for an accommodation with Fascism and that their rulers did not see
in it any principles of action hostile to the interests
of privilege. It is not true to say that they were deceived by the Fascist dictators, save in so far as
they were the willing accomplices of the deception.
No one can read the details of the relations between the Fascist leaders and the governing classes
of Great Britain and France in the years before
the war without the conviction that those classes
felt a common interest with Fascism in its anti-
democratic attitude, above all in the example it had
given of the disciplining of the working-class institutions. How else can we explain the contrast in the
treatment of the Russian Revolution and the Fascist
revolutions? How else can we explain the enthusiasm
of those classes for General Franco, their willing-
ness, even, to take the strategic risks of his victory?
Admit that some of the more extreme practices of the
Fascist powers embarrassed them by reason of the
indignation they aroused, yet there was never any
question of such a *cordon sanitaire* about the Italian
or German doctrine as they had sought to draw
round the doctrines of the Soviet Union. Fascist

speakers in Great Britain were occasionally sen-
tenced to minor penalties for insulting behaviour;
there was never any question of the dramatic conspiracy trials such as the Communist leaders experienced. It was known for years that the Fascist
movement in Great Britain was financed from abroad,
but that never aroused, among the privileged classes,
the resentment felt at the similar relation between
the British Communist Party and Moscow. Great
aristocrats and eminent business men went without
criticism to Nürnberg, and they usually returned
to voice their ardent confidence not only in the pacific
intentions of the Nazi leaders but in the virtue of
their social experiments; while the pilgrimage to
Moscow was, significantly enough, almost wholly
confined to workingmen and intellectuals. There
are few men of prominence in the Conservative
Party who have not lavished eulogies upon Mussolini; in the light of the evidence, it is impossible
to explain their ignorant enthusiasm except upon
the basis of sympathy with the way in which he had
disciplined the workers of Italy. The observer of
governing-class opinion in Great Britain in the years
before the war is, I think, honestly bound to record
the sober view that nothing in the antagonism of
either Hitler or Mussolini to democracy aroused any
general indignation against them until they threatened vital British interests. At that point came the

[53]

drift to war and, with it, the identification by that governing class of the protection of British interests with the preservation of democracy. But that was essentially a rationalization produced by the psychology of war, the discovery by the governing class of the necessary basis of national unity. The "evil things" Britain was driven to fight were discovered by its rulers after war began; they were not perceived by them while Fascism was preparing war.

Much the same conclusion will, I think, be evident to the student of politics in pre-war France, with the important difference that the clarity of French political discussion made the issue there more explicit than it was in Great Britain; the *haute bourgeoisie* of the Third Republic was far more determined to be done with democracy than was the case with ourselves. The tendencies that were vaguely present in Great Britain went deeper in France. That is shown, in part, by the degree to which an avowed acceptance of Fascist doctrines already permeated the high command of the army, a considerable section of the upper civil servants, and the "Two Hundred Families" before the war; it is shown, in part, also, by the character of the support won by organizations like de la Rocque's Croix de Feu; it is shown, in part, further, by the fact that, already on February 6, 1934, Fascism was powerful enough to make French parliamentarism totter on its foundations; and, finally, it is shown in part by the intensity of the policy of appeasement as it was symbolized by politicians like Bonnet, Laval, and Flandin. It is significant that, as I shall show later, the triangle of interests through whose co-operation Fascism has in each instance destroyed democratic institutions was already active in France before the outbreak of war. It is also significant that these interests were jeopardized by the advent of the Popular Front in 1936, and that its social reforms, built on the rapid growth, in that year, of trade-union organization, were met by a deliberate strike of French capital which succeeded in overthrowing the Blum government. Exactly the same class sought a *modus vivendi* with Fascism in France as in Great Britain; and its efforts failed because Fascism demanded concessions which would have been incompatible with the maintenance of France's position as a great power. Those who sought to avoid the challenge to Fascism in France were essentially the men who recognized that its defeat involved the risk of a European revolution in which all privileged interests would be in hazard. They did not seek to avoid it in order to defend democracy from attack; the blinding light thrown on their motives by the capitulation of 1940 makes it evident that it was for capitalist privilege and not for democratic institutions that they were concerned.

It is in the light of these years before the war that
we must interpret the policy of the British and
French governments in the period in Great Britain
up to the overthrow of the Chamberlain government,
and in France up to the end of the Third Republic in
June 1940. Both governments exhibit the same character. Neither had any positive policy for peace to
put forward. Neither showed any capacity to realize
the scale of preparation the war required. Neither
was able, save for British action at sea, to take the
initiative in any theatre of war. Neither showed any
capacity not merely to arouse neutral enthusiasm for
its cause, but even to make its own people imagi-
natively aware of what was at stake in the conflict.
The British government never seriously attempted to
evoke from its people the effort the power of war demanded. That is shown decisively by Sir John (now
Lord) Simon's Budget of April 1940; it was far more
concerned with the economic aftermath of the war
both by the expenditure it envisaged and by the
taxes it imposed than with the organization of victory. It announced, of course, that it was fighting for
democratic institutions. But practically every pro-
nouncement that it made, and, even more, the men
and the measures upon which it relied, made it manifest to the masses that the democracy it proposed to

defend was that of September 3, 1939. It was seeking, in a word, to preserve the contours of the past; it was not seeking to discover the necessities of the future.

There is a significant statement of Mr. Chamberlain's in this connexion which throws a flood of light upon his mind. In a broadcast of June 30, 1940, he explained that he did not think the workers would put forth the effort that victory required until the bombs began to fall on Great Britain. What are the real implications of that remark? It is, surely, that Mr. Chamberlain had no confidence in the power of the Britain he symbolized to evoke from them the energy that victory required until the ravages of war had made them passionately angry. He had no confidence in that power, and his own lack of confidence was paralleled by his own inability to elicit the confidence either of the trade-union leaders or of the Socialist leaders. They refused, unanimously, to join his government; they declared that as they had distrusted him before, so they distrusted him after, the war. He stood to them as the symbol of a world they sought to change in its fundamentals; internationally, not less than domestically. They did not believe that, so long as he was the head of the government, they could secure from him the changes they sought; he embodied their denial. He was not willing to seek the terms upon which the collaboration of the

[57]

workers could be secured, because that would have involved him in the demand for parallel and proportionate sacrifices from the forces of privilege he represented. He would not ask for those sacrifices, because they meant a change in the social foundations of Great Britain. He was not prepared to be the sponsor of such a change. It was because of that unpreparedness, above all, that he had been the supreme "appeaser" in the pre-war years; Munich symbolized his whole philosophy of life. *Quieta non movere* was the quintessence of his doctrine, and he had no conception of the fact that totalitarian war demands the remaking of the commonwealth. He was fighting, let me emphasize again, for a past to which the declaration of war itself had already, though he did not know it, made it impossible for Great Britain to return.

That discovery was not made by the British people until the revelation of unpreparedness and inefficiency in the Norwegian campaign; up to that point the tempo and substance of Mr. Chamberlain's mind seemed to fit the tempo and substance of the war itself. But the Norwegian campaign made evident that the formidable power of the enemy foreshadowed the recurrence of similar disasters if he remained in power. The accession of Mr. Churchill to office, in collaboration with the Labour and Liberal Parties, transformed the situation. It did so because its coincidence with the invasion of the Low Countries

made evident the possibility of defeat and because
the scale of effort that possibility required involved
a philosophy of action which Mr. Chamberlain was
not in a position to supply; he was not in a position
to supply it because it was alien to all the principles
he held in respect. To defeat the menace of the dictators it was essential to appeal to the dynamic of
democracy. To appeal to that dynamic it was necessary to make the war against the dictators in the fullest sense a people's war. But to make the war a
people's war it was necessary to ask for their sacrifices on the supreme condition that they were not to
be used merely to preserve the *economic and social
status quo*. A democracy that is to wage totalitarian
war must end economic and social privilege as the
price of victory. It must, that is to say, take large
steps toward the transformation of the capitalist basis
of its economic foundations to a Socialist basis.

For it is compelled to organize the economic life
of the nation as the necessary condition of totalitarian
warfare. To do so on the side of labour it must secure
from the workers the suspension of the protective devices they have developed for the safeguard of their
interests, and it must prevent any stoppage in the
flow of production during the war. It must, further,
satisfy the workers about their standard of living. A
capitalist democracy can do these things only when
the whole mind and heart of the workers are in the

[59]

war effort, and this will be so only when the sacrifices demanded of privilege seem to the workers proportionate to those demanded from labour. But this at once involves paying regard to the social objectives for which the workers have organized their political power. It means, in fact, that the effective dynamic of democracy depends upon realizing in a continuous way those objectives which the workers identify with social justice.

It was this effort that the Chamberlain government never made, mainly because it rejected the outlook which called for it. Mr. Chamberlain, indeed, perhaps only half consciously, was waging a war, after September 3, 1939, on two fronts. On the one hand, he was seeking to break Nazi aggression; on the other, he was seeking to preserve all that he could of Great Britain as it was on that date. What the Norwegian campaign foreshadowed, and what the battles of the Low Countries and of France decisively demonstrated, was that the two objects were incompatible. And this was true because, as I have argued, in a period, like our own, of economic contraction the principles of capitalism and the principles of democracy are in contradiction with one another. A capitalist democracy which wishes to mobilize its full resources in war must therefore either widely extend the frontiers of democracy in order to secure the full support of its workers, or it must suppress its demo-

cratic character in order to be in a position to coerce
the workers into obedience to the will of its government. But this latter it cannot hope to do without in-
curring the risk of civil war and, thereby, of defeat.
If it does not make an experiment with the dynamic,
it risks defeat once more, because, as Mr. Chamberlain found, it cannot mobilize the resources exacted
by the scale of totalitarian war. And under a parlia-
mentary system, a government at war will not sur-
vive the conviction that it lacks imagination, energy,
and efficiency. That was the conviction formed by the
public of the Chamberlain government during the
Norwegian campaign; its inevitable result was Mr.
Chamberlain's defeat.

I add here that I reject the view which attributes
the failure of the Chamberlain government to the desire, even after war had begun, for appeasement at
any genuine opportunity which presented itself. I
believe that Mr. Chamberlain, after September 3,
passionately desired the utter defeat of Hitler, but I
think that desire was incompatible with the objects
for which he wished that defeat. For those objects
required methods and changes incompatible with
his philosophy. That is why he could win the support
of the Labour Party for the war, but not for either
his method of waging it or, in any but a nominal
sense, his conception of a satisfactory peace. The
dynamic upon which he relied was that of the old

[61]

social order, in which the emphasis was rather on privilege than on democracy. That this was so could be seen from the relation of the trade unions to production under Mr. Chamberlain; they remained formal rather than substantial. It could be seen in the taxation he imposed, in the social legislation he was prepared to approve, in the intensity with which he clung to the men who had approved of the Munich settlement as his instruments. Mr. Chamberlain, I am convinced, wanted not less than the most ardent of his critics the defeat of Hitler, but the way in which he approached the problems of capitalist democracy made it impossible for him to understand, much less to secure, the conditions necessary to victory.

The defeat of France, I suggest, emphasizes the same lesson, if in an infinitely more tragic way, for the collapse of the Third Republic will prove, in perspective, one of the major calamities of modern history. Its explanation lies in three directions. Partly, the will of the French government to resist operated throughout in the environment of men who, in the name of privilege, preferred capitulation to the price of victory. Partly, the years of the peace had produced a France so riven by internal differences that few of its leaders had grasped the proportions of their problem or made the preparations to cope with it. Partly, from the outset of the war, the rulers of France did all they could to arrest the dynamic of the people. It was not only that the arrest of the Communist leaders—a measure which the Communists themselves did everything to render inevitable—cut off from the workers those most capable, at the moment of capitulation, of organizing resistance to it. It was also that the prevention of free criticism made the masses the victims of an illusion. The coming of defeat was so sudden that they could not escape from it before they were the helpless victims of surrender. And it is clear now that for a considerable period before the actual surrender the Lavals and Baudouins were negotiating its arrangement. They were prepared to accept victory on the old terms; they were unwilling to organize it on the new. Swift defeat broke the will of a High Command which, to recover any prospect of continued resistance, would have had to appeal to the revolutionary will of the people. Men of the opinions of Weygand and Pétain were unwilling to embark upon an adventure which was a denial of all their philosophy. They combined with the high officials whose experience had led them to identify the interests of high finance with those of the commonwealth, like Baudouin, or who were, like Laval, nothing so much as its commercial travellers, to effect a *coup d'état*. They broke the democracy of France partly in the hope of winning mercy from those conquerors who, over years, had proved themselves without mercy to

[63]

their opponents and partly to rescue from its wreckage some shadow of the privileges they believed the evolution of democracy to endanger. They killed France in the fear that capitalist power might be lost if she reorganized for future victory.

Each day in the unfolding of the French tragedy confirms the truth of this analysis. The France of 1789 is transformed at a stroke into a Fascist wraith as dependent upon the whim of its conquerors as Denmark or Czechoslovakia. In the futile hope of placating them the makers of the Pétain regime destroy all the symbols and institutions upon which the greatness of modern France was built. The Fascist technique of repression is evoked as a necessary discipline of the people. The *Führer-prinzip* is eulogized in complete forgetfulness of the fact that its previous application in France led directly to the Revolution of 1789. The only security the regime possesses is that provided by the power of the enemy upon whom it depends. It has no roots in tradition, in popular will, in foreign support. Born in a defeat from which it cannot recover unless its enemy is overthrown, it lacks even the possibility of discovering a dynamic. It cannot satisfy its people for the simple reason that the more its implications are understood, the more that people will be outraged by them. It cannot satisfy the friends of France to whom French liberation is, above all, escape from its results. It cannot even satisfy the enemies of France, since, if it grows in power, it becomes a threat to their security. And even in these first pathetic days of its history, it is provided with an emigration, that is to say, men whose main objective will be to overthrow it. A German victory, to put it in a sentence, means the slavery of France to purposes it cannot share in defining and will not be permitted to challenge; a German defeat means the revolutionary overthrow of the Pétain regime. And with that overthrow there will disappear the capitalist privileges it was the aim of the regime to preserve. Rarely in history will the betrayal of a great purpose have brought with it so swift a revenge.

v

In the defeat of the smaller democracies by the Fascist dictators there is no material for surprise. All of them lacked the resources which would have enabled them, as independent states, to give meaning to the principle of neutrality; and when they followed the example of the major democracies in abandoning as idle the hope of collective security they sealed their fate. Their experience is significant, above all, of two things. It is the proof that a serious League of Nations cannot be built upon the principle of state sovereignty. That principle means that the vested interests of each part of such a League triumph at any critical moment over the total interest of the whole. But the proper inference from this is not, I think, the simple one that enthusiasts for the League are inclined to draw: the belief that had statesmen in Geneva only displayed a little more fidelity to the idea of the League, shown a little more goodwill on its behalf, it would not have broken down.

The inference of the enthusiasts fails to take account of two things. It omits, in the first place, the clear contradiction between the idea of the League as an organized society and the idea of a sovereign state which cannot be bound to any rule of conduct by that society against its will. It fails, in the second place, to realize that the great states (which alone possessed sovereignty in any effective sense of the term) refused to surrender that sovereignty because its retention was essential to the protection of what they regarded as their vital interests. And those interests, when analysed, will always be found to be directly related to the internal distribution of economic power. Peaceful change, in fact, was not possible in an organized and continuous way as between the great states, because, as soon as it touched those interests regarded as vital, it would have meant a change within each in the internal distribution of economic power. That, in its turn, would have had an important, sometimes a decisive, influence upon both privilege and the standard of life in each state.

From this angle, behind the façade of the League,

post-1919 politics was as much a struggle for power
as it was in the pre-1919 epoch. The League could
not maintain the peace, because, once the sovereignty
of its individual members was retained, it lacked the
authority to impose its will upon them; when, indeed,
any of them exercised its sovereignty, in any fundamental sense, the League had no will. And the struggle for power in the post-war world went on unchanged because the economic needs of the world
were in contradiction with its political institutions.
These, in their ultimate conformation, protected a
body of vested interests which, as Germany, France,
Great Britain, the Soviet Union, Italy, Japan, were
prepared to fight rather than give way on any interest
deemed fundamental. And each body organized as
a state could mobilize in its support the national sentiment of the territory over which it exercised control.
With economic crisis, these vested interests not only
needed protection from invasion—hence the effort
at autarchy in the post-1919 period—but they needed
also expanding markets to cope with the profitable
disposal of the immense volume of production which
technological development had made possible for
them. Without these possibilities, they were bound
to confront large-scale unemployment, and the experience of these years was the inescapable one that
its continuance over any long period threatened the
security of those vested interests and, of course, the

[67]

privileges enjoyed by those who owned them.

Herein lies the modicum of much in the argument that this is a war between the satisfied and dissatisfied powers, or, in a more favoured terminology, a war of rival imperialisms. Granted the internal distribution of economic power in Germany and Italy, within the market area under their control, they could not, in the post-1919 conditions, maintain a way of material life satisfactory to their peoples; which meant, in turn, that under a democratic system those peoples would use their political power to alter that internal distribution to their own advantage. The breaking-point between capitalism and democracy in those states came earlier than in France or Great Britain because their internal accumulated wealth and the external advantages, such as colonies, they could exploit threatened the owners of privilege at a much earlier stage. The first action of those owners was to co-operate in the destruction of the democratic basis Italy and Germany had achieved. But the permanent suppression of democracy was possible only if the new regimes then founded could satisfy the masses by giving them, in the long run, economic security and the hope of a better standard of life. Within the framework of Fascism, they could not do this except by expansion. But expansion, in the situation they confronted, meant conquest. They had therefore to embark upon large-scale military

preparations at least adequate to a possible challenge
from those whose rights they attacked, and, as events
showed, ultimately from France and Great Britain.
More than this: while they prepared for conquest,
they had, so far as they could, to postpone the challenge they would in the end be compelled to make
lest they be overwhelmed before the gamble of conquest seemed a legitimate risk.

They had, further, both with their own people and
with their potential rivals, to prepare the psychological ground for their adventure. This was a complicated task, since their manœuvres, under the conditions of power-politics, compelled their potential
rivals also to rearm and thus threatened within them
the power out of their greater resources at once to pay
for rearmament and to maintain the delicate balance
between capitalism and democracy. The methods
adopted were undeniably brilliant. At first they made
only those claims which their rivals, for a number of
reasons, were unwilling to deny. While they were
organizing their preparations, they posed as the enemies of the Soviet Union. That pose enlisted on their
behalf the sympathies of all who believed that the
existence of the Soviet Union was a threat to the
private ownership of the means of production. Simultaneously, they insisted to their own people on the
validity of their claims to extended power while they
wooed the privileged classes outside with their pro-

testations of peace. And with this Machiavellian dualism of outlook there went a deliberate and wholesale corruption of all the forces in the rival states that were capable of being corrupted, with the result that their half-concealed purposes bewildered and disunified the capitalist democracies up to the very moment when they were ready for the challenge. When that was flung down, it was clear that their ambitions were in fact unbounded and that they could not defeat the capitalist democracies without depriving them of those material conditions in which the basis of democracy could be maintained.

In this sense, the critics of Great Britain and France who have denied that, in the phase of the war which ended with the surrender of France, these powers were fighting for democracy were guilty of a half-truth. Great Britain and France each confronted their rivals with not one purpose but two. To their privileged classes, they were fighting to preserve the delicate equilibrium of capitalist democracy, an equilibrium in which, as the policy of Mr. Chamberlain and M. Daladier showed, the emphasis was on the capitalism rather than on the democracy; but both Mr. Chamberlain and M. Daladier could honestly hold that they were fighting for democracy for two reasons. First, if either was defeated, his country would no longer be able to maintain a democratic system in the sense in which each of them understood that term; and, second, for reasons I shall explain in the next chapter, in comparison with the Fascist systems, no serious observer could honestly deny the reality of the democracy in capitalist democracy.

But those in Great Britain and France who were not associated with the privileged classes did not mean by democracy what Mr. Chamberlain and M. Daladier meant. They were not profoundly interested in the maintenance of that capitalism which the two Prime Ministers regarded as vital. Yet they fully understood that, if France and Britain were defeated, their democratic foundations would collapse and with that collapse, as the overwhelming mass of them believed, the possibility of successfully transforming the capitalist basis of democracy into a Socialist basis. They were fighting, like Mr. Chamberlain and M. Daladier, on two fronts. On the one hand, they passionately desired the defeat of Fascism, since they recognized in it the vital enemy of working-class interests; on the other, they wished to extend the frontiers of democracy, during the conflict, into the social and economic spheres, because they believed that the more egalitarian the society, the profounder would be the resolution of the masses to win, the greater, therefore, their capacity to ask them for the sacrifices which, it was increasingly evident, the massive strength of Fascism would demand for vic-

[71]

tory. They supported, this is to say, the waging of
war against the Fascist powers; they had no doubt
that their challenge must be fully met. But their very
different conception of the implications of the democratic idea meant that they could not, to take the
British instance, support the methods by which Mr.
Chamberlain waged the war, and they were bound
to be suspicious of the peace he would make if circumstances enabled him to be the architect of
victory.

Therefore, up to the German attack on the Low
Countries, at any rate, the partners in the enterprise
of war against Fascism were in a dilemma. Each attached a different emphasis to the elements in the
struggle upon which they were jointly engaged. Neither could convince the other that acceptance of his
particular emphasis was desirable. Neither could seek
from the electorate a refreshment of his political
strength because the stress of the conflict made such a
consultation effectively impossible. When the Norwegian defeat came, the vividness of the danger compelled the Labour Party in Great Britain to join
forces with Mr. Churchill in a new National Government; to have refused would have been to invite
party suicide and national defeat. In the new com-
bination, there was no doubt that the balance of the
emphasis was far more toward those elements to
which the unprivileged attached importance than it

was under Mr. Chamberlain. There was certainly, and at once, a notable change in the energy and imagination with which the war effort was conducted, a more vivid sense of the dangers that had to be overpassed. Certainly, also, the fact that the appeal to the workers for effort and sacrifice was made by men in whom they had confidence changed the whole psychological perspective in which the appeal for their energy could be made. And this is true even when full allowance is credited to the sense, which grew daily with the disasters in France, of how near the feet of Great Britain lay the abyss. The greater the danger the nation confronted, the more it seemed able, in the new direction, to rise to the height of its problems. To all appearance, the next phase of the battle with Fascism seemed capable of producing, even when Britain confronted it alone, a dynamic proportionate to its magnitude.

It seemed capable of producing that dynamic; the question was what were the conditions upon which it would be produced. For the task of organizing the defeat of the dictators is, on any showing, a tremendous one. It was not only that, for all effective purposes, the British Commonwealth stood alone. It stood alone against an enemy able to devote to its attempted destruction all the weight of its resources at a time when those of Great Britain were still considerably distant from their maximum potential. It would be compelled, therefore, for no inconsiderable period to fight on the defensive; its people could not be nourished on that sense of going forward which the power to take the offensive implies. It would have to endure under constant threat of attack, with at least the high probability of actual invasion. And while on the defensive, it would have to watch the grim spectacle of its enemies consolidating their hold on the conquests they had completed, the spectacle of a famine-ridden continent powerless to help itself until its conquerors began to face the possibility of defeat.

The Churchill government, that is to say, has a problem of which it is futile to underestimate the dimensions. It has to organize for that offensive which alone can give it the possibility of victory. It has to maintain and intensify the resolution of its own people as the means to that organization. It has to persuade the peoples of the European Continent not to fall into the apathy of despair by offering them evidence enough to penetrate beyond the poisonous miasma of Fascist propaganda that there is one unbreakable fortress of democracy upon whose future help they can rely. And there is the final stage in which, organized to take the offensive, the British government can, as its effective basis, organize wholesale revolt among the enslaved peoples against their Fascist conquerors.

Where We Stand Today

These are the tasks for which the dynamic of British democracy has to be mobilized; and, from any point of view, they are heavy tasks. They can be accomplished only by leaders with a faith in the common people and a full power to win their confidence in return. That faith, no doubt, can be manifest in the spoken word, and it is already evident that, in Mr. Churchill, the British people have found a leader whose greatness in utterance matches the greatness of the issue. But, in the realm where men now contend, the real test of faith is in the decisions it impels. Their character is the key to victory. They only have the ultimate power to maintain resolution and create hope. The road to a victory for democracy lies not merely in the affirmation of its historic procedures, but in the effective enlargement of the ends for which these are used. It is in its power to organize the enlargement of those ends that the British government will provide the true measure of its determination to overthrow the tyranny of Fascism.

CHAPTER TWO

What Fascism Is

I

THE Fascist state, whether in its Italian or in its German form, offers a certain rhythmical pattern of which the significance is unmistakable. In each state, it is important that the Fascist leaders were able to build a mass movement; but it is important, also, that they could not, under its auspices, attain power. Their seizure of the state was in both instances the outcome of a body of understandings, unknown to the rank and file of the movement, between the Fascist leaders, on the one hand, and the heads of the army, the civil administration, and big business, on the other. In both instances, also, these latter assumed that they were invoking an ally whom they would be able to dominate for their own purposes. In both cases, also, they were deceived. They assumed that they were calling in the Fascist leaders as junior partners in the effort, from the angle of privilege, discipline, and order, to confine the ambitions of the masses to reasonable proportions. They found, in fact, that they had put themselves under masters

[76]

whose sole care was the perpetuation of their own power.

It is notable, also, that both in Germany and in Italy certain psychological and economic conditions of a similar kind facilitated the growth of Fascism as a mass movement and produced leaders of a similar kind who used similar methods for their purposes. In both, the war had produced a deep sense of national humiliation either, as with Germany, through actual military defeat or, as with Italy, because the fruits of her victory did not seem proportionate to her effort. In both, also, peace brought profound economic crisis to peoples with no long or profound training in democratic traditions. In both, also, the war left, in conjunction with economic crisis, not only a great army of unemployed, but also a great mass of *déclassé* adventurers, *condottieri* of the pen and the sword, restless, inured to habits of violence, unable to make a success of their lives within the framework of the societies in which they lived. In both countries, the masses, in part, at least, fired by the example of the Soviet Union, felt bitterly the insecurity of their condition and the inadequacy of their standard of life, while the depth of their dissatisfaction seemed to their masters a growing threat to the privileges they enjoyed. In both countries, the traditional form of state had ceased to command respect because it could no longer maintain that unity of the national mind upon which social order, in terms of government by discussion, obviously depends.

Both in Italy and in Germany Fascism begins with the formation of a little band of adventurers, whom no one takes very seriously and who seem chiefly concerned to draw attention to their own importance. But both in Italy and in Germany the little band has at its head a demagogue of genius. Its influence grows because it is able to exploit every grievance of a diseased society. It is careful to have no coherent doctrine. It is luxuriant in its promises. It offers the assurance of a renewal of that national pride which has been humiliated. With the deepening of economic crisis, the band grows into an army, disciplined within itself, violently undisciplined to its critics and its enemies. Those who join it are for the most part the *petits bourgeois,* discontented with their lot, the youth frustrated in opportunity and eager for adventure, the ex-officers who cannot accustom themselves to a small place in the placid routine of an ordered civilization, psychopathic men, like Ley and Streicher, who cannot fit the rules their vocation imposes upon them. Those who support it are the men and women to whom any promise of order and regeneration is the prospect of relief from the insecurity and feverish indiscipline of the times. The little shopkeeper is enthusiastic because he is told that he will be freed from the competition of the big department stores and the co-operative movement. The big industrialist, like Thyssen, is attracted because the movement's hostility to Marxism is a lever of attack against the pretensions of the trade unions and the Socialist movement. The farmer is interested by the promise that he will be freed from the tyranny of the mortgages under which he groans. The professional man is moved by its anti-Semitism in the degree to which, as lawyer or doctor, he is inclined to attribute his failure to the Jews. The ex-serviceman hears with gratitude that he was not defeated in the war, and that the wrongs of Versailles will be redressed. Italian Fascism and German Nazism could have been prevented from growing into a serious menace only if the governments of Italy and Germany had been able to remedy the grievances of which they were the expression.

But the depth of the economic crisis made that impossible, and it seemed as though the traditional wisdom of the old state-order was at a discount. In each society, therefore, an arrangement was effected between the forces of privilege and the Fascist movement by which they agreed to share power upon the basis that democratic institutions would be suppressed. Each had been privately assured beforehand by the Fascist leaders that they had no interest in the popular slogans by which the masses had been attracted to their support. Each was convinced that, once democratic institutions were in abeyance, the discipline of the masses could be restored; in those circumstances, privilege would be safe, the conditions of successful business enterprise would be resumed, the possibilities of revenge for defeat or disappointment in the war of 1914 could be organized. The privileged, therefore, agreed by what was, in both the Italian and the German instances, a conspiracy to place the Fascist leaders, as their agents, in possession of the state-power. Each found, as soon as those leaders had entered upon its possession, that they in fact repudiated the agency and became the principals in the undertaking.

The first step of the Fascist leaders was the destruction of all movements and organizations which were a contingent threat to their power. The trade unions, the co-operative movement, and all rival political parties were brought to an ignominious end, and their funds were usually confiscated. A reign of terror was introduced in which the known enemies of Fascism were murdered, sometimes by judicial assassination, or imprisoned; and the terror was so successful in preventing any effective organized opposition that it became a permanent part of the Fascist system, built upon a massive secret police and concentration camps in which the infliction of torture became a regular feature. Wholesale dismissals took place of all officials of whose loyalty the Fascist leaders were uncertain; this served the twofold purpose of strengthening their hold upon the administration and of enabling them to satisfy their trusted followers with jobs. All the organs of propaganda—the press, the radio, the theatre, the cinema—came under the direct control of the new rulers; except, therefore, as secret conspiracy and, therefore, as crime, criticism of their policies became impossible and the whole population was subject to those doctrines only which they wished to impose. All educational institutions were similarly purged and remodelled to their purposes. Local government was deprived of any popular basis, and those who presided over it were made responsible, on a hierarchical principle, ultimately to the leader of the state. Judicial institutions and the criminal code were similarly revised for the same end. The party apparatus for all practical purposes became the state, for the leaders of the one became the rulers of the other. Though a formal legislative assembly was maintained, its only function was to meet occasionally to listen to the leader's pronouncements, since in him was concentrated all executive and legislative power. From time to time, also, a plebiscite was taken to approve some dramatic step of the leader; as it usually resulted in a vote of approval which varied around ninety-five per cent of the electorate, it is, I think, a legitimate inference that it was less a free expression of opinion than a measure of the intensity with which terrorism had consolidated the leader's power. For it is important to remember that neither Mussolini nor Hitler had, before his *coup d'état*, been able to command a majority of the electorate for his policy. After the *coups*, each was even able to obtain a majority of approval in the concentration camps in which his victims were confined.

The problems which each dictator confronted when he assumed power were, above all, three in number: there was the problem of consolidating his power, there was the problem of economic grievance, and there was the problem of restoring national prestige. The first was solved, quite simply, by terror, more severe and brutal in the case of Hitler than of Mussolini, but in each case an intense terror which paid no regard to either the person or the property of its victims. The solution of the economic problem is a more complicated story, and I want here to emphasize only one aspect of the way in which it was dealt with; and I shall emphasize the German experience, since its consequences and, indeed, its psychological success were far more important than in the Italian case.

As I have emphasized, it was, above all, economic crisis which brought Hitler to power, and the mass support he gained in that crisis came, again above all,

from the unemployed. To maintain his power, therefore, his central problem was, so far as he could, to
abolish unemployment, for that would remove the
main danger which confronted him. But to do so
would still leave unsolved the recovery of national
prestige, and upon his ability to handle that successfully his relations with the army depended; it must
always be remembered, in assessing his policy, that
in the first years of his power the Reichswehr was
the one element in German politics which could have
overthrown him at any moment, the element, moreover, the strength of whose traditions it was most
difficult for him to overcome. What Hitler did was
to solve both problems at a stroke by embarking
upon a gigantic programme of rearmament. From
the angle of the unemployed, this was equivalent to
an immense state programme of public works of ever-
increasing tempo. It therefore rapidly absorbed the
skilled unemployed, first in the heavy industries and
then in the mass of the subsidiary trades which
supply the equipment of the modern mechanized
defence-force. And since the state controlled the conditions of labour, he was able, at the same time, to
utilize fully the resources of German industry. The
shortage of those raw materials for which Germany
depended upon imports enabled him, further, not
only to control all foreign trade, but also, largely
through the ingenuity of Dr. Schacht, to develop a

system of barter whereby, in the first years of rearmament, the weaker countries living by the export
of primary materials were drawn ever more closely
into the German economic orbit, since their systems
of production were largely geared to each other's
needs.

But this rearmament also had the effect of tying
the army closely to Hitler's interests. It was given a
pre-eminence in the state by the place offered to its
needs in the economic programme, and its prestige
was immensely enhanced by the glorification of war
and the army's traditions in the educational programme. No doubt a price had to be paid for the
army's support. There is a sense in which the mas-
sacre of June 30, 1934, was part of that price; so, too,
was the apology for the "accidental" assassination of
General von Schleicher; and there is some evidence
that the army was at the outset dismayed by the
daring of Hitler's ambitions. But as stroke succeeded
stroke with ever more resounding success, the army
yielded its allegiance to Hitler far more fully than
it had ever done to his imperial predecessor. No one
had ever given it so powerful a place in society; no
one had ever, either, so completely freed its demands
from the possibility of criticism; no one, above all,
had ever put before it plans of such immeasurable
ambition. In Hitler's dreams for the army there was

not merely the material for avenging the defeat of 1918; there was the prospect of a military glory which promised careers to the soldiers beyond any hopes they had dared to entertain.

And with the fulfilment of militarization there came also the restoration of the national prestige. German demands after 1933 and, even more, after 1936 did not meet the curt reception they had encountered under the Weimar Republic. Behind them, increasingly, was a mailed fist entitled to threaten war and, it was possible, prepared to make it. The more complete Hitler's subjugation of Germany, the more willing was the outside world not only to submit to his annexations, but even to try to find a basis for believing his word or explaining away each deception that he practised. They were shocked when he abruptly left the League of Nations, but they tried not to scrutinize too closely the meaning of his abandonment of it. They were shocked when he adopted conscription, but they hastened to explain to themselves that this was, after all, an internal German decision. There was a moment of danger when he refortified the Rhineland, but easy-going British statesmen, after suitable verbal rebuke, assured the agitated French that, after all, German territory must be the subject of German decisions. They were shocked when he organized the murder of Dollfuss, but they limited their indignation to verbal protests. They were shocked when, in conjunction with Mussolini, he intervened in Spain and lied without hesitation about his intervention. They were shocked when he occupied Austria and annihilated its independence, but their anger had no sequence in deeds. They were dismayed when he demanded the Sudeten districts of Czechoslovakia, but they made an elaborate pretence of persuading themselves that to yield to his demand was not obvious betrayal but the recognition of a just claim. Only when, on March 18, 1939, he took over the whole of Czechoslovakia did the world admit to itself the vastness of the threat he implied to its safety. But by that time not only was he in a position to deal with any challenge it might offer; he had conquered the mind of most Germans by giving them a status in which all Europe deferred to his every whim. A speech of Bismarck's might be a matter of diplomatic speculation; a speech of William II was sure to be a matter for diplomatic apology; but a speech of Hitler's was an event upon which the whole world waited breathlessly, since he had given it the conviction that its fate depended upon it. German diplomacy, under him, might be the bully's technique, but, from being nothing, he had made Germany the most feared nation in Europe. He told its people that this fear measured the degree to which he had restored its self-respect, and so profound was the hypnosis under which it lay that millions of Germans, especially young Germans, were ready to believe him.

Nor does this end his achievement. The Marxian critics of Hitler argue, as they have argued of Mussolini, that he represents the betrayal of democracy in the interest of finance-capitalism; this, they have urged, is the essence that he symbolizes. There is the real truth in this that without the support of big business he would not have attained power, any more than Mussolini would have done, and that his suppression of the historic defence-mechanisms of the workers' standard of life has accrued to the interest of big business and is the main reason why his regime aroused enthusiasm among the privileged classes abroad. But this explanation omits the vital fact that it is true of him, as, in a less degree, also, it is true of Mussolini, that he controls big business hardly less than he controls the working class. German industry was not permitted by him to resume the conditions of the free market. Profits were strictly controlled. If labour standards were forcibly lowered, it was under Fascist, and not under business, direction. The whole functioning of business enterprise, as much as that of labour, was geared at every point to the imperative needs of the rearmament plan. Its requirements at every point determined what the business man could do with his capital. He exchanged the irritations of constant interference by labour for the irritation of constant subjugation to the Nazi purpose. He might be rich and powerful; he was free from the uneasiness of Socialist threat. But there was no sort of doubt but that Hitler was the master of big business and, as Thyssen's experience made clear, that it must live its life on the terms he imposed upon it.

For him that position had important advantages. It enabled him to argue to the mass of Germans that the economic system in Germany was free from the weakness of "pluto-democracy" in that it rigorously limited the right of capital to unlimited profits. It enabled him to urge on the business men that the devotion of surplus profits to rearmament was ultimately to their advantage, since rearmament would facilitate conquests which would offer the prospect of boundless prosperity. It enabled him, further, to show the army that the whole economic forces of German society were geared to the service of the purpose it fulfilled. It enabled him to urge upon his own devotees that this intensity of state-control was, in fact, the fulfilment of the Socialist aspect of his programme. And to all Germany he could say that the domination of Europe his rearmament promised would one day open up a vista of endless riches, if only they had the patience and the self-sacrifice to wait for victories it would bring.

[88]

What Fascism Is

All the world, as Dr. Ley has said, was to work for Germany once the system had achieved its conquests.

It is perhaps worth pausing here for a moment to point out the profound resemblance between Hitler's system and the general characteristics of the mercantilist period. In each instance there is private ownership of the means of production, but in each instance, also, that ownership is set in the context of a state-authority which regards it as the purpose of that ownership to serve its own power. Private fortunes are therefore subordinate to public necessity as this is envisaged by those who operate the state. Since the state is regarded as standing above and beyond individuals, since, indeed, their meaning is derived from their relation to it, the state assumes complete control of all economic activity. It does so because the sole interest it has is in the development of its own power. It is in terms of that power that it regards the economic life of other communities; it seeks so to influence it, by arrangement if possible, by compulsion if necessary, that they are also geared, as the North American colonies to Great Britain before 1776, to the increase of its power. In crisis, the regulation this involves goes so far that it becomes difficult to distinguish state-capitalism from state-socialism except by the attention that is paid to the needs of the workers. The standard of life depends upon the state; the level of profits depends upon the state; the direction of investment depends upon the state. So, too, do foreign trade, the right to work, the right to found and develop a business; the rights of property are extended or extinguished according as they are regarded by the rulers of the state as serving the increase of its power. Where feudalism, liberal capitalism, and democratic socialism have been interested always in an economics of plenty, mercantilist policy, whether before the age of Adam Smith or in that of Hitler and, though less fully, that of Mussolini, is interested in an economics of power. To that end, plenty is subordinate, and if its realization interferes, as with Hitler's programme of rearmament, with the achievement of power, plenty is ruthlessly sacrificed to its claims.

II

Much ingenuity has been employed by scholars to find an appropriate intellectual pedigree for Fascist doctrine. Here, its sources are traced to Kant; there the responsibility is fastened upon Hegel; we are bidden to remark the influence of Nietzsche or Machiavelli, of Sorel or Pareto, on the substance of the totalitarian idea.

I believe all such efforts are fundamentally mistaken, and that it is of the first importance to recognize this fact. For they all rest upon the assumption that, like the philosophies I have enumerated, Fas-

cism is a logical system capable of rational analysis
and of rational defence; an assumption, be it noted,
which implies that if Fascism were shown to be ra-
tionally indefensible, its foundations would have
been cut from under it.

I think this intellectual approach an erroneous one
for a number of reasons. It is important, first, that
the makers of the Fascist movements were fundamentally uneducated men, wholly unconcerned with
the building of a logical system. They were men
who, on their own confession, were at once driven by
ambition, avid of power, and unable to make a success of life in the society to which they belonged.
From the outset of their careers they denounced its
rules; they hated them because those rules stood in
the way of their success. They protested against
them, whether, as with Mussolini, by joining the Socialist movement or, as with Hitler, by becoming
part of a less organized band of its assailants. Each
gathered around him a band of kindred spirits, the
soldier without a job, the *déclassé* intellectual with
no regular routine of work, the disappointed teacher,
and so on. Around a central group there gathered
an army of the underworld, the men who in America
would have grouped themselves about the racketeers.
In the feverish conditions of post-war Italy and Germany, with their profound insecurities and massive
discontents, there was no difficulty in finding an audi-

[91]

ence. They were careful not to put forward any coherent programme; that would have tied them down
to a body of concrete purposes. Their technique was
the simpler one of exploiting grievances and insisting that they had sovereign remedies for them. The
grievances were whatever men were capable of hat-
ing upon a scale wide enough, and with an intensity
deep enough, to win support. They personalized their
enemies in the sure knowledge that the masses are
always interested by concrete symbols of hate. The
enemies are the Jews or the Bolsheviks, the capitalists or the Socialists, the bankers or the owners of the
big department stores. They insist on the weakness
of a government that might have been victorious and
was defeated. They promise to renew the past glories
of the nation, to give them an extension they have
never before possessed. They bid their followers be
strong; they encourage them to be violent and applaud it as strength. Their tactic is, in both cases, that
of the street-corner orator who has the evangelist's
power of making his audience drunk with emotion.

It is important to recognize three things in this
tactic. It has no doctrine; it nourishes its power on
the emotions of helpless grievance and angry hate;
it promises revenge upon those who are represented
as the makers of grievance and hate, and promises
immediate redress both against them and against
what they have caused. The promises were from the

outset impossible, partly because they were utterly
contradictory and partly because, in their reckless
immensity, they were really promises to lift the curse
of Adam from the sons of men. But they were a tactic
cunningly devised. They came to peoples discontented and frustrated, and smarting under the sense
of intolerable humiliation. Everyone could find some-
thing there which seemed to apply to his own case;
everyone felt sure that the pith of the movement was
the remedy of his own particular grievance. As movements, neither Italian nor German Fascism won the
direct support of the solid and the successful. It won
over to its side the discontented and the despairing,
the bewildered little man, afraid of life and eager at
all costs to believe the incantations of these weavers
of spells who had a magic formula for everything.
It was colourful and dramatic; association with it
filled many a life that would otherwise have been
empty. It appealed enormously to the young, for it
offered risks and it gave a romantic career and an
easy road to power. It had in it the call of a challenge
to the dubious manœuvres of the Italian politicians,
who, however the complexion of the government
changed, always seemed in the end to come back to
Giolitti, who changed nothing; or to the clumsy respectability of the Weimar Republic, the child of defeat and the parent of failure. Its challenge competed
favourably with the middle-aged stodginess of Ger-

[93]

man Socialism of which, after all, Weimar was the dubious child, or even of the German Communists, with their repudiation of national traditions, their complicated textual disputes, their bewildering changes of leadership, above all, perhaps, their call, on a foreign model, to a further revolution which seemed to promise only further insecurity.

Economic crisis and political disappointment fed the movement. It began to attract the attention of those to whom democratic institutions seemed a threat or a frustration—big business, the army, the high functionaries of the civil service, the aristocracy. These began to notice its possibilities, to form their underground connexions with it. They commenced cautiously to finance its treasury, to discuss whether, in appropriate circumstances, it might not prove useful. Private assurances were forthcoming that its Socialist proclamations were only a façade, necessary to deceive the masses. The essence of the movement, so they were informed, was above all its hatred of Bolshevism on the one hand and its yearning for national regeneration on the other. The privileged interests which took these soundings had no doubt that these were their own objectives. They agreed that they were desirable. They saw that they meant the restoration of order and the disciplining of the masses. They became steadily more convinced that they could use the Fascist leaders for their purposes.

[94]

What Fascism Is

It would mean the destruction of democracy. But it would mean security for their privileges and relief from the torment of fear that Italy or Germany might move to revolution. They struck their bargain with Fascism in the confidence that their mercenaries were restoring to them the mastery of the state.

Here, of course, is the sense in which the Marxists are right in insisting that Fascism is the expression of capitalism in decay. But the analysis which stops there omits the vital factor in the equation. Privilege brought the Fascists to power as partners, and it is, I am confident, certain that without privilege they would not have attained power. But it is fundamental to understand that the forces of privilege were as much deceived in their acceptance of Fascism as the masses who supported it. For the privileged wholly omitted from their consideration the character of their partners. They did not understand, until it was too late, that it was the outlaws whom they had brought to power.

No emphasis upon that outlaw character of Fascism can be too great. It is inherent in the life-history of the men who dominate its ranks. Not only were they failures in a regime under the rule of law. Not only did they have contempt for the masses who accepted a rule in which they got most of the toil and little of the gain of living; they had contempt for the masses because, as outlaws, they had rejected a rule which normally confined them to poverty and failure. But they hated, also, the forces of privilege because it was these which had made the rules that condemned them to failure. To accept a partnership with them would mean an acceptance of rules against which, as experience has shown them in their own lives, the revolt they themselves had symbolized was certain, sooner or later, to be provoked. To accept any rules meant a government under law; that was a denial of their own inherent nature. It meant the imposition of a system in which traditions, conventions, habitudes, might easily make them superfluous to the forces which had called them in as their mercenaries; from that superfluity might easily develop, if not their deposition, at least their reduction to a status where their power was purely formal.

As outlaws, in fact, the Fascist leaders, half deliberately, half—I suspect—unconsciously, had the wit to perceive that the day on which an ordered and coherent society was established would be fatal to them. They did not, therefore, propose to allow it to come; they had not hewn their way to power in order to surrender it. The only values they understood, the only values, indeed, which had meaning for them, were those which consisted in the exercise of power by themselves. If it be asked for what end they proposed to exercise power, the answer is for

[96]

the sake of power itself. Any other answer would have involved them in subjection to rules which made power the recognized servant of an end beyond itself, and that recognition would have been a denial of their own nature as outlaws. To take an obvious example, it would have been like Capone settling down to be an ordinary and law-abiding citizen of the United States; he might have been more comfortable, but he would not have been Capone. Gone would have been the risks and the excitement and the romance; above all, the intoxicating sense of power would have gone. They had hewn their way to supremacy by the defiance of the rules. That was how they had made the masses afraid of them. That was how, also, they had compelled the forces of privilege to court their alliance. They lived by insecurity, violence, the chaos these compel. They could not subdue themselves to a settled place in an ordered cosmos without ceasing to be themselves.

It was no use appealing to them on the grounds of reason; they represented the triumph of unreason because as outlaws they were the foes of all settled principle. It was no use appealing to them in the name of the law; for them there was no law but their own will to power. It was no use to urge upon them the splendour of peace; their power had been the outcome of war, and peace meant its end. Jus-

[97]

tice, mercy, kindness—all these were the values of
the weak who shrink from pride in the exercise of
power. There was no price that could be paid to
them which would compensate for subordinating it
to rules. They could be offered wealth, but they
had already learned that power makes wealth in
their ascent. They could be offered honourable fame,
but the whole world, as it was, was discussing
them and, enjoying the adulation of conquerors,
they had, as outlaws, no use for honour. And if the
regime of virtuous principle was offered them, they
had, again as outlaws, for them the final answer that
the man with power makes his power itself virtue
and that the virtue of the life they had come to
dominate was merely a deception by which privilege
controlled the masses.

Their view, in fact, was the simple one, derived,
I must again emphasize, from their experience that
as fear and deception had gained them the state
so fear and deception would maintain them in possession of it; and they had no other end than this
maintenance. And from this end all that they have
done follows with almost the directness of a syllogism.
They had to establish a regime of terror within that
their enemies might be stricken with impotence.
They had to destroy any organization, whether of
the Left or of the Right, which might even con-
tingently become a source of possible challenge to

their authority. The very fact, this is to say, that they had no other end but power compelled them to make a totalitarian system, to remould society, thereby, in their own dreadful image. They had to do so for just the same reason that it is the first instinct of the gangster to reach for his gun. For whatever they did not control was for them an explicit threat to their power; they could not know whence the threat might come; they must, therefore, be the masters of everything lest they discover, too late, that they had lost all. Working-class institutions, religious institutions, economic institutions, political and cultural forces—all these they had to reshape to their own purpose and control by their own men. For everything outside the ambit of their authority might live a life of its own, have a spirit of its own, deny, in the end, their ethos, which was simply their own unchallengeable right to power.

Their terrorism, therefore, was not an accidental excrescence which would decline as they grew into responsibility, for they could not grow into responsibility without becoming the exponents of a system of values incompatible with the recognition of their right to power. Their terrorism, no doubt, sprang from various motives. They pillaged the Jews not so much because they were afraid of them as because they needed a scapegoat upon which to lavish the hates they had called up. They imprisoned Socialists and Communists because these were the most likely sources of hostility and opposition to them. They deprived the legal code of its precision and coherence because with these they risked its devotion to the purposes of their enemies; after all, none knew better than they that a legal code may be twisted into a means of attack upon a regime. They militarized the educational system and fed the children of the nation into the ranks of the party because in no other way could they break so completely the hold of the old German traditions of decency and respectability upon the younger generation. They attacked and imprisoned and drove into exile that great mass of men who had been the standard-bearers of German culture because in no other way could they announce so decisively their breach, as outlaws, with the central stream of civilized thought. Their attitude to reason, indeed, could not have been more permanently or effectively symbolized than by the burning of the books. The literature they thus committed to the flames was, in large part, the creator of the values they had come to deny.

"A people," wrote Edmund Burke, "must have some compensation for its slavery." Fear alone, as the outlaws understood, would not have satisfied the masses, for there is a point beyond which despair becomes the parent of frenzy. The Fascist lead-

ers, therefore, had to grapple with the problem of
unemployment; they recognized that, without the
registration of success in this realm, they could not
consolidate their hold upon the state. I have already
noted the skill with which they met this problem.
By relating it to their need to dominate the army,
they did, in effect, three things. They found work
for millions for whom revolt would mean a threat
to security at last attained, often after long years
of misery; the security might be won at a dimin-
ished standard of life, but the psychological importance of even such security as a means of obedience
must not be underestimated. For there accompanied
it what may fairly be termed an industrial martial
law which made the worker dependent, through
his employer, on the party machine for the continued
means of livelihood, with the omnipresent possibility
that evidence of protest against his conditions might
be equated with disaffection and lead him to a concentration camp. The second result was to link increasingly, as the scale and pace of rearmament
proceeded, the interests of the defence-forces with
those of the Fascist leaders. This, clearly, strength-
ened those leaders' hands both negatively and posi-
tively; negatively because it drove a wedge between
the business interests, seeking for the restoration
of economic security, and the defence-forces, which
could support the business interests only by sacrific-

ing the growth of their own prestige. Here, of course, was an admirable instance of that division of possibly hostile forces which is always the basis of a dictatorship's strength.

But the third consequence of the rearmament programme was the most important of all, because of its immense international repercussions. The Fascist leaders had to revive the national prestige; for them that was synonymous with revenge for past humiliations, a revenge which might be made the more impressive by being linked to new conquests. The obvious advantage of this was that it permitted the use of national feeling to conceal domestic grievances likely to be felt deeply, such as the reduction in the standard of life for the masses; the technique is at least as old as the *Politics* of Aristotle. But it had the further benefits that, by causing international uneasiness, particularly when, as with the militarization of the Rhineland, there would be wide agreement upon its justice, it created a sense of national danger and thus a further recognition of the need for national unity. Naturally enough, as the scale and significance of Fascist rearmament became understood abroad, it provoked counter-rearmament among the nations which might be affected by it. This created exactly the atmosphere of international tension which the Fascist leaders desired. In the first stage they could use it to unite their friends by

insisting, as with Hitler, that they were only demanding their just rights; while they divided their
enemies who, above all, did not want war and had
an uncomfortable feeling that whatever the manner
of its making the claim had some real justice behind
it. And their enemies felt, too, that if they met the
claim by action the result would be a general breakdown in Europe in which only the enemies of
privilege would reap the benefit. They thus not only
showed their hesitation and divisions; they also
added enormously to the prestige of the outlaws by
giving them victory after victory without a battle.

In the second phase, the outlaws passed to bolder
ambitions. They were the leaders of poor nations;
they would be the leaders of rich ones. They lacked
living space, market opportunities, adequate access
to raw materials. They denied the validity of the
international status quo. They insisted upon their
right to a new dynamic of imperialism which would
redistribute the sources of the world's wealth. At
first they were rarely taken seriously. Their rhetoric
about their mission, or their historical claims, or
their racial superiority, the comparison between their
youthful vigour and the effete antiquity of their
rivals, were taken to be no more than propaganda
for domestic consumption. They might, it was assumed, praise war and prepare all the gestures of
war. But the rulers of the capitalist democracies

[103]

could not bring themselves fully to believe that the Fascist leaders really meant war. They had bad manners, no doubt; after all, they were the parvenus of statesmanship. The old diplomatic methods, skilfully used, would appease their appetites. They might thunder and gesticulate, but they could not be so utterly irresponsible as to will war.

Any careful scrutiny of the utterances of men like Mr. Chamberlain in Great Britain or M. Daladier in France will, I think, make it clear that until the seizure of the rump of Czechoslovakia in March 1939 this was the real background of their thought. They did not know the scale of their opponents' preparations; they could not believe that the historic might they themselves represented would, in the last resort, be actually challenged; they felt confident that before their own people the Fascist leaders would always, before the clock struck twelve, come to some rational arrangement. One can, I think, glimpse that despairing faith of Mr. Chamberlain and M. Daladier in some ultimate flicker of rationality in the Fascist leaders in their hesitations during the last twenty-four hours of peace. To them the idea of war itself was horrible, and the problems it would leave behind would be almost beyond the power of man to solve. It would be totalitarian war, in which what would be at stake would be civilization itself. They could not believe that any statesmen could be gamblers so wicked or so reckless.

What they had never understood was the simple fact that the Fascist leaders were not statesmen but outlaws; the rational considerations by which Mr. Chamberlain and M. Daladier were moved meant nothing to them. They did not care about the fate of civilization; by instinct and experience they were the enemies of civilization. They had won power; they wanted to maintain power. They had sought to maintain it by building an immense military machine upon which, as a going concern, the life of their peoples had come to depend. They had reached a position where, to maintain themselves, they had literally no alternative but to win victories. Without them the material basis upon which they depended would collapse, and the psychological basis also. For the outlaw leader cannot afford a defeat, since defeat for him is the shadow of the law his whole ethos denies. Like the gangster in the United States, he must have spoils to divide among his dependents, or give way to another who can get them. The whole structure of his authority is built upon the assumption that it cannot be successfully challenged. Once it is so challenged, all those who have accepted his will are encouraged in their turn to challenge it. The defeat of the outlaw is the end of the outlaw.

So that when the capitalist democracies would not continue the policy of appeasement, the Fascist leaders made war in precisely the same spirit as the outlaw who knows that surrender to the police is fatal to his authority over his gang. The considerations which moved the leaders of the capitalist democracies meant nothing to them at all. If they won, they had spoils undreamed of to divide, and they would be merciless in dividing them. If they lost, they would be no worse off themselves than if they accepted the policy of peace, since that would carry with it the certainty of revolt against their power. They were bound, therefore, as outlaws, to the gamble of power. While the gamble lasted, its very immensity gave its exercise a character of far deeper intoxication than any they had so far experienced. And they knew, what the capitalists of the democracies were only slowly driven to understand, that they had an extraordinary chance of success. They knew the intensity of their own preparations; they knew, also, the deficiency of their opponents'. They knew, and had built upon, the inner contradictions of the capitalist democracies; they could count upon the fact that their unity for conflict would, on the intense scale which totalitarian war demands, be far more difficult to achieve and far more difficult to maintain—as the tragedy of France has made evident—than their own. They knew, also, that they

could count upon scruples in the conduct of operations by the capitalist democracies by which they
would not be bound, which, therefore, would add
immensely to their swiftness of initiative and pro-
fundity of striking power. I do not say that Hitler
entered the war without forebodings; and it is clear
enough that Mussolini had many of them. But I do
say that in neither case were the forebodings those
of a civilized person. Their criterion was simply and
solely the rightness of their calculations in estimating
their chances of success. Once they were satisfied
with these, they entered upon the conflict with com-
parative light-heartedness. What for their enemies
was a threat to civilization was for them the promise
of a new world with the attractive horizon of unlimited power.

III

This contrast between the moods of the leaders of
the respective combatants is of enormous importance.
One of the most striking features in this war is that
it has nowhere produced among the common people
who are fighting it any temper of exhilaration; that
has been noted of Germany and Italy by careful
neutral observers, and it is certainly true of the
French and of the British. And in the capitalist democracies the attitude of the leaders has suited the
temper of the common people. It has been the sombre

determination of men who are fighting an epidemic, not the joyous zest for battle of men who revel in a great opportunity. They have taken a choice not sought, but forced upon them. However passionately they desire victory, they know that its price still, on any view, will render it less desirable than the peace they were anxious to maintain. It is certainly my own sober judgment that no war in modern history has aroused less of the martial spirit than this war. That has been true of its inception and its continuance; it is still the spirit in which those who weigh its character seriously approach its possible termination.

This attitude must be set, not over against that of the peoples in the Fascist states, but certainly over against that of their leaders. The whole nature of their speeches has been set upon two interconnected planes: on the one hand has been the threat of ruin to the enemy states unless they gave way to the Fascist demands, on the other has been the almost ecstatic contemplation of the power of which they will dispose, the loot there will be to divide, when the victory has been won. As already mentioned, one discourse by Dr. Ley, the leader of the German Labour Front, explains that on the conclusion of peace the whole world will have to work for Germany, which will then enjoy untold riches. Underlying what they have to tell us are certain unmistakable pictures of the future they envisage. Germany is to be a master-people, to whom all other peoples will pay tribute. The economy of other states will be adjusted to the needs of the German national economy. The liberty and independence of other states will be set by their obligation to accept the domination of Germany in, at least, Europe. And none of this means a recognition that the common people of Germany are to be freed from the tyranny which now controls them, even when the might of Germany is established beyond challenge. The general principles of Fascist power-politics remain not less applicable internally after victory than before. The victory of the German and Italian states, that is to say, remains essentially a victory of their rulers; the common people fulfil the only purpose for which they are fitted by being the instrument of that victory.

It is, indeed, clear that the necessity of a continued militarization remains after victory as before. For not only are the conquered to lose immense territories; the alteration of their national economies to fit the needs of German wealth means their reduction to vast areas mainly producing, under Fascist supervision, the primary commodities that Germany requires. They will, in fact, be colonialized, on that mercantilist model I have already noted, for German benefit. And since the result of this process is bound to be, even beyond the costs of war, a grave reduction

in their standards of living, their military control by
the Fascist powers will be necessary in order to prevent them from indulging in the luxury of revolt
against their slavery; it is notable that German comment, even before the peace terms, insists that France
has been a bad neighbour for a thousand years and
that her people must be reduced beyond the possibility of resistance. The obvious advantage of this
scheme is threefold. It offers the hope of pacifying
the German people by offering them the prospect of
largess. The great armies it envisages as being maintained imply the continuance of large numbers of
important posts for Fascist supporters. The tension
upon which the Fascist leaders rely for their authority is continued even after peace. For the advantages
held out to the German people by the scheme depend upon their blind obedience to their leaders. The
alternative is revolt and therefore war, with the prospect that successful revolt will deprive them of all
the fruits of domination.

It is, surely, in its very essence a racketeer's dream.
It is like nothing so much as the attitude of the American gangster who is compelled continually to extend the theatre of his operations lest some rival be
tempted to move into its occupation. And it is important to note that it cannot, in fact, stop at the
conquest of Europe. It is already aware of the threat
to its power implied in the existence of a free and

independent America. It has already been driven to take steps to thrust forward into the American scene. Were it to be successful in Europe, it would, indeed, have no alternative. For as long as America was free from its habits, its slaves in Europe would be bound to look to America as the author of their emancipation. And what holds of America holds, also, of the Soviet Union. That experiment, whatever its crimes and blunders of procedure, is built upon ideas incompatible with Fascist ambitions, and it has, as in the wheat-fields of the Ukraine and the oil-fields of Georgia, sources of primary material wealth which the Fascists will neglect at their peril. They were, indeed, in one sense right in their angry insistence that they were the profoundest enemies of Marxism. They recognized in it, with wisdom, a system which, because it built power on principle, was ultimately incompatible with their authority. In the short run, rather than the long, they cannot feel safe until they have settled their account with Moscow.

The immanent necessity of the outlaws, in short, is their need to conquer the whole world. They are unsafe so long as there is a free people anywhere, for its freedom may, as they are fully aware, infect their slaves. They are unsafe even, as again they are fully aware, while there is anywhere an independent tyrant whose rule is not subordinated to theirs; for them he represents a constant suspicion that in their

search for security he may be the source of their
downfall. The logic of their position, in fact, compels them to search after power in the world outside
Germany and Italy by the same methods as they
have won it within them. They must be all or nothing, simply because they are bound to fear that, unless they are all, they may on any day become nothing. They are bound to seek the destruction of any
rival and independent power simply because its idea
may become fatal to their uneasy poise at the apex
of their pyramid. That, of course, is why they already
seek to foment disturbance and corruption even in
the societies to which they protest the ardour of their
goodwill. Indeed, the very vehemence of their protest is a measure of their fear of those societies. That
emerges, interestingly enough, in the comparison one
can make, for example, between what they say of
the United States to itself and what they seek to im-
press upon their own people about the United States.
For the first, there is the constant assurance that
they have no interest in its fortunes, that a Nazi-
dominated Europe would respect the integrity of the
American Continent as it would expect to be re-
spected, that American energy and inventiveness
command their admiration. But their own people,
aware of the lack of American sympathy for the Fascist cause and uneasy that its immense resources
should be available to Great Britain, are informed

[112]

at the same time that there is no reason to fear America, that any help it might give will arrive too late to count, that it is, in any case, disunited and rotten with corruption, and, above all, that when victory has been won in Europe there will be a stern accounting with the American foe.

The inference which must be drawn is, I think, inescapable. It is implicit in the internal history of Fascist evolution; even more, it is explicit in the history of Fascist war upon the capitalist democracies. It is the inference that between Fascism and its opponents there can be no compromise. For accommodation in politics is possible only between men who have the great ends of life in common. They then share the same values, they can reason together about more or less. But it is the essence of the outlaws' position, first, that they utterly deny any end their opponents can recognize as valid, and, second, that they deny altogether any values their opponents are prepared to respect.

They deny, first, any end their opponents can recognize as valid. For what they seek is complete and unassailable power, and that involves them in the position that their opponents cannot have ends of their own; they must be reduced to the position of instruments of Fascism. Nothing, surely, proves this more clearly than their treatment of France after capitulation. They warn its leaders that they are not

satisfied even when the men of Bordeaux have remodelled the French regime in the Fascist image,
and, on that pitiful basis, considered how they may
protect those French interests for which the surrender was made. For they fear that the very conception
of "French interests" already implies some pale
wraith of French independence, and, at once, as I
have argued, because independence is a threat to
subordination, they are bound to regard it as a future
source of disturbance to their power.

They deny altogether any values their opponents
are prepared to respect. For, as outlaws, they reject
any conception of values external to, or independent
of, action which ministers to their power. They are
bound to do so, once more, because their central position is the simple one that their might makes their
right. And their conception of their might is an ex-
clusive one. They cannot admit partners to share it,
since they know that divided power makes the loca-
tion of mastery a dubious matter. For them, as Car-
lyle said, the only ultimate question between two
human beings is: "Can I kill thee, or canst thou kill
me?" So, too, in their judgment, between states.
Since, therefore, all politics is a matter of either their
life or their death, the only values admissible are the
values that secure their life. Right, in this conception, means that behaviour which ministers to their
security; wrong is that behaviour which threatens it.

[114]

What Fascism Is

The Fascist ethic (if, indeed, it may be dignified by that name) is therefore simply a strategy of the expediencies which suit the state. But since the state is the Fascist Party, and this, in turn, is reducible to its leaders, it follows that their view of what is expedient is alone decisive; and their view of what is expedient is set by the simple issue of whether it adds to or detracts from their power. Any values which offer a different purpose or are built out of a different experience are thus, from the angle of their objectives, no values at all.

It is the naked gospel of what William James called the "bitch-goddess" success. My point is the simple one that it provides no ground for discussion with those who preach it. It provides no ground, because as outlaws they are not bound by any agreements they may make save to the point where, for their own advantage, they choose to be bound. That has been the clear record of Hitler and Mussolini in the years of "appeasement." Each demand was the last demand; each annexation was the last annexation. Each demand and each annexation proved, in fact, no more than the prelude to the next. Those who were appalled by the shameless cynicism of this procedure committed a fundamental error. For they were applying moral tests of behaviour to the Fascist leaders which had no meaning for them. They were assuming that the Fascist leaders were not outlaws,

[115]

that they were concerned in preserving that maxim *pacta sunt servanda* which is the cement of civilization. They utterly failed to see, first, that if the outlaws preserved that maxim they would cease to be outlaws, since they would then have admitted a rule of conduct to which their own behaviour must be subordinate; and, second, they utterly failed to see that, once the rule was admitted, the outlaws would have confronted problems they could not solve. But the day on which they cannot solve their problems is, because they are the votaries of the "bitch-goddess," the day on which they begin to lose their power.

It follows from this that there is no alternative for the enemies of Fascism but its complete overthrow, and this means, in the circumstances we confront, nothing less than complete defeat in war. It is a hard conclusion because, clearly, the strength of the resources at the disposal of the outlaws means a bitter struggle of painful sacrifice. But the years of "appeasement" provide the answer to any who find this conclusion too hard. To leave the outlaws in possession of their authority is to make it certain that they will use it only to begin again the battle for ultimate power. To argue that some accommodation might put them in a position where they may be overthrown from within omits to notice that it assumes that the outlaws will accept an accommodation which leaves their enemies with the prospect of their overthrow. Of any such accommodation I think there are two decisive things to be said. First, the Fascist leaders would not accept any such accommodation unless they judged that they were in grave danger of military defeat; in that case, on experience, it is the part of wisdom for their enemies to make assurance doubly sure by making the defeat a final one. And, secondly, if the accommodation were made, the fact that the Fascist leaders were left in possession of the state-authority would mean, again on experience, that they would exploit it for no other purpose than to destroy those forces within their society which might be able to organize their overthrow. By so doing, that is to say, they would not only regain their authority, but they would be compelled, in order to effect its reconsolidation, to embark again exactly on that career of conquest which, as I have argued here, is an essential condition of their maintenance of internal power.

One may go further. The argument for accommodation rests upon an unstated belief that the experience of war, especially if it foreshadows defeat, will persuade the outlaws to a more rational outlook upon the universe. I see no evidence for this view. It is not only that it assumes that the outlaw is converted by experiencing the very condition he has called into being by the deliberate necessities of his system. It is, also, that it is contradicted by the way in which the outlaw wages war. For that way reveals that the more difficult the situation he confronts, the more ruthless are his procedures. The more complete his successes, the more relentlessly are the mechanisms of his apparatus applied. It is not accident that the first arrival in each occupied country has been the representative of the Gestapo; it is symbolical that the method used to compel acceptance of his rule in Poland was a travelling gallows, complete with the actual bodies of the victims. We cannot deal with the outlaws except upon the understanding that the only sin they recognize is weakness and that, for them, every virtue in their opponent is a proof of his weakness and therefore of his sin.

So that we have to rule out the possibility of compromise; you cannot meet unreason with reasoned discussion. We have tried that method and it has brought us to the verge of disaster. You can deal with the outlaw only by force; as he seeks to break your will, so you must seek to break his. That means, therefore, military defeat to the point where his power over his subjects is broken beyond renewal. The defeat must be decisive; his collapse must be an abject one. Except in these terms, there is the danger that we leave the poison of the infection he has caused in the society he has been able to dominate. There must be no chance that the German people may be persuaded again that it was betrayal and not defeat which brought about the downfall of their rulers. There must be no risk that we make distinctions between the outlaws and offer compromise to some that we deny to others, that, for example, we seek an accommodation with Göring that we refuse to Hitler or with Grandi that we refuse to Mussolini. Perhaps the most inept of all the approaches to the problem of the outlaws has been the attempt to make these distinctions; "Göring," said Sir Nevile Henderson, "may be a blackguard, but he is not a dirty blackguard." If the inference is that we can build an enduring peace upon elegant refinements of this kind, that only shows how deeply the representatives of the privileged classes in capitalist democracy have the poison of appeasement in their systems.

We have to be very clear that there is no modification of Fascism short of the full acceptance of democratic procedures which can form the basis of an enduring peace. More than that, we have to be clear that democratic procedures can be safely operated only by men whose bona fides about their validity is beyond dispute. For politicians who have "ifs" and "buts" in their attitude to democracy will, consciously or unconsciously, sooner or later conspire against them. That is the reason, for example, why the enthusiasm of eminent British Conservatives for Dr. Rauschning makes little impression on the Left in England. Dr. Rauschning is a member of that Right in Germany whose fear of the implications of democracy led them to risk the use of Hitler as their agent. They turned against him rather because his purposes went beyond their own than because they objected to his attack on democratic procedures. They came to understand that he symbolized the nihilism of the outlaw. But as long as his nihilism was directed only against the foundations of the Weimar Republic they did not object to it. Their conversion to the proclamation that he was dangerous came only when they began to see that he whom they had chosen as their instrument had in fact made himself their master. To ask them to rebuild a democratic Germany would be like asking the House of Lords to foster the strength of British trade unionism.

This is, indeed, a relation which we have to watch with very peculiar care. There are many Englishmen who, after a period of blindness, have come to recognize the Fascist danger, and seek for the overthrow of its leaders. But it is important that many of them think of that overthrow essentially in terms of a body of men who have seized power. Defeat and discredit them, they appear to argue, and the task will have been done. We can then deal with a new set of leaders, whether in Germany or in Italy, with whom accommodation is possible. Mr. Duff Cooper, for example, has spoken hopefully of a palace revolution in Germany. The military, it seems, are to overthrow Hitler and his associates, and an authentic monarchy of the traditional kind is to be reestablished. With the men of such a system, we are told, negotiation is possible. Here is the possible lever to peace.

Men who think as Mr. Duff Cooper does ignore the dynamic of war, above all, the dynamic of totalitarian war. Their approach to Fascism is the simple and unsatisfactory one which assumes that a body of bad men seized the state and, out of their insatiable ambitions, willed war when they could have willed peace. They recognize the need to defeat the war-makers, but they ignore altogether three things. They ignore those through whom the Fascists came to power. They ignore the significance of the mass support which persuaded privilege to give the Fascists their chance of power. They assume that when men rather like themselves have replaced the Fascist leaders all will be well, since they are conscious of their own dislike of war. They assume, further, that since men rather like themselves, both in Germany and in Italy, will also dislike war, it can be repelled by a simple joint effort of will. All of us, in the days before the war, heard discussions of this kind. "The fate of Europe," we are told, "rests on the will of one

[121]

man." The causes of this extraordinary dependence were rarely examined by those who thought in this way.

But no one understands Fascism, or can deal with it, who thinks of its problems as consisting of the replacement of bad men with bad ambitions by good men with good ambitions; affairs in politics are not subject to simple interpretations of this kind. Unless we understand that the Fascists came to power because the privileged classes in a capitalist democracy in the last resort preferred capitalism to democracy and were therefore prepared to take the risks of Fascism, we shall miss the central problem it presents. Unless we understand, further, that the mass support of Fascism came, overwhelmingly, from little men, frustrated, bewildered, insecure, unhappy, because of the failure of capitalist democracy to solve their problems, again we shall miss the central problem. Unless, finally, we ceaselessly remember that neither Hitler nor Mussolini willed war in the sense of consciously choosing its tragedies in preference to those of peace; that they chose war because the objectives Fascism drove them to desire were incompatible with peace; that they were in a position where they had to aim at those objectives because the alternative was their downfall; that they had attained this position by collusion with the representatives of privilege who collaborated with them in the de-

[122]

struction of democracy; again, without this clearly in
our minds, we shall not understand Fascism. All this,
politicians like Mr. Duff Cooper completely ignore.
They think of peace as a negotiation made with men
who represent above everything that privilege of
which the fears and embarrassments gave the outlaws their opportunity. What guarantee of endurance
could there be in a peace so made?

And because war with Fascism is totalitarian war,
politicians like Mr. Duff Cooper ignore altogether its
dynamic. The world that emerges from the peace
will not be the world that entered the war. It cannot
go back to the confused contradictions which led it
into conflict without inviting an anarchy so profound
that the very idea of reason will become meaning-
less to mankind. We all say—not least emphatically
politicians like Mr. Duff Cooper—that we are fighting Fascism for liberty and democracy. But very
rapidly we have got to make up our minds who are
to enjoy that liberty and democracy for which we
are fighting. Is it all the inhabitants of the world or
only some of them? If it is all of them, it becomes
clear at once that, whatever the future organization
of society, it cannot be modelled upon the framework of the present organization, for it is precisely
the present organization, with its confused contradictions, that has led us into this war. And if it is to be
liberty for only some of the inhabitants, then we are

entitled to know the principle upon which the sheep
are divided from the goats.

We are entitled to know the principle and, whatever it be, it must involve the rejection of liberty and
democracy simply for those who can get power and
keep it when they have got it; that is the politics of
power because of whose implications we find ourselves fighting Fascism today. Clearly, if it is that,
the conflict is one between two cruel irrationalisms
the result of which makes very little difference to
those excluded from liberty and democracy. And if
it is not that, then we are entitled to know either that
the liberty and democracy are to be all-embracing
or that the principle of exclusion is one that is ra-
tionally satisfying to those excluded as well as, and
not, I think, less than, those favoured by inclusion.
For, otherwise, those who have taken the masses into
this war, by whatever high-sounding rhetoric they
may conceal their purposes, have taken them into it
to fight for a liberty and a democracy confined in
their benefits to a very few, and that is, in effect, to
take them into it to fight for capitalist democracy.
On this view, they are identifying capitalist democracy with civilization. On this view, also, the labour
leaders who are pledged to a Socialist reconstruction
of our society will find themselves fighting the very
men with whom they are now in partnership as soon
as Fascism has been defeated. And at that stage the

clear danger emerges that those in a capitalist democracy who fear for their privileges in the conflict will suppress the democracy rather than risk the privileges they enjoy under capitalism.

I think that danger very real. I think it real because one is bound to be suspicious of men who can give noble names to evil things without any sense of the confusion in their minds. That confusion runs like a continuous thread through Lord Lloyd's statement of our war aims, in which he records his enthusiasm for Italian Fascism; and that statement has been endorsed by Lord Halifax, who tells us that in this war we are fighting for Christianity. The Prime Minister tells us that we have one aim only—victory. But we are compelled to ask: Victory for whom and for what? It is surely obvious that until we know with real precision the answers to these questions there is the chance that, as in the war of 1914, we shall merely change the balance of power for a period, leaving untouched the root issues out of which conflict itself emerged. As I have insisted here, Fascism is above all the rule of the outlaws and thus the denial, in their interest, of all values. Therefore, the way to fight it successfully is to make clear beyond peradventure the virtues for which we are fighting. For I do not think many Englishmen would fight a battle of this magnitude, over any considerable period of time, merely, to take two obvious examples, that the profits of Rio Tinto should come to the privileged classes in Great Britain rather than to those of Germany or of Italy, or that the profits of the jute mills of India should go to the one rather than to the other. The subject of this world war is the right of mankind to the values inherent in the democratic way of life, or it is a war in which the conflict of values has no meaning. But if it is the first, as I believe, then our leaders have the obligation to assure the triumph of those values.

That means, I am wholly clear, the utter defeat of Fascism. For behind all the phrases which it uses to conceal its nature, whether, as with Hitler, it is "the common interest before self" or, with Mussolini, "the conception of the state as an absolute"; whether we describe it, with Sir Oswald Mosley, as "the creed and morality of British manhood" or, with Dr. Goebbels as the "socialism of duty," we know that it has in fact no doctrine at all. That is why, in his notorious letter to Bianchi, Mussolini could demand the production of a philosophy for Fascism "within the two months between now and the National Congress"; "Italian Fascism," he wrote,[1] "now requires, under pain of death, or, worse, of suicide, to provide itself with a body of doctrine"; that is why, also, all attempts to give real substance to the corporate state have so lamentably failed. That is why Hitler could

---

[1] *Messaggi e Proclami*, 1929, p. 39.

write[2] of the state as "the organization of a community homogeneous in nature and feeling, for the better development and preservation of its type, and the fulfilment of the destiny marked out for it by Providence," even while he could explain the futility of his definition in the letter to the industrial leader Fritsche in which he explains that "there are catchwords like 'Down with capitalism!' etc., but these are unquestionably necessary, for under the flag of 'German National,' or 'National' alone, you must know we should never reach our goal, we should have no future. We must talk the language of the embittered Socialist workmen . . . or else they wouldn't feel at home with us. We don't come out with a direct programme for reasons of diplomacy."[3] The racialism which accepts Italians and Japanese as honorary "Aryans" when expediency so dictates; the revival in religious forms of old German mythology; the sudden adoption by Mussolini, after sixteen years of power, of anti-Semitism as a cardinal part of this programme; these, and the many similar expedients, are the proof that Fascism has no doctrine, but only slogans which give to the actions the leaders propose to take that basis in popular support they believe it advisable to secure. And the sole pur-

[2] *Mein Kampf,* English edition of 1939, p. 195.
[3] Quoted in E. A. Mowrer, *Germany Puts the Clock Back,* p. 150.

pose of their action is the consolidation of their power.

It is a power which has become absolute over their own people and seeks to become absolute over the world; it is the supreme modern example of Acton's classic dictum that "absolute power corrupts absolutely." And just because it is absolute, it is beyond the capacity of principle to penetrate; the logic of absolute power is that it claims to be its own self-justification. Those, therefore, who have embarked upon the task of its destruction must not only state the principles for which they propose to destroy it, but, hardly less, for whose benefit the principles are to be applied. They have the duty, not only to formulate a programme of ends, but to prove that the means which are to realize those ends are relevant to the purposes they avow. For when the leaders of a nation ask the masses to die for a dream, the men who risk their lives are entitled to know on whose behalf those leaders dream. They cannot be asked to march to a battle the survivors of which do not share the fruits of victory. That is to be the instrument of a purpose they are not permitted to share. It is to exchange the slavery imposed by the outlaws for a condition that may easily become a slavery once more.

◇◇

CHAPTER THREE

What Are We to Do Next?

I

FROM events so passionate as those in which we are involved it is not easy to detach ourselves. Yet, viewed in perspective, their meaning is clear enough. We have reached a revolutionary phase in the history of our civilization because the character of our political institutions contradicts the possibilities of our economic achievement. Scientific discovery has given us the means of a vastly more abundant life. But to realize that abundance we need, not least in the international sphere, a revolution in our political institutions and in our ways of thought. Between that abundance and the changes its realization requires there stand the vested interests of privilege which fear the effect of that revolution upon themselves. At the extreme, their fear is reflected in the surrender they have made to the Fascist leaders. These, to preserve their power, have struck at privilege elsewhere in the hope that its conquest may give permanence to their authority. But the manner and the time in which, as with ourselves, the Fascist leaders have struck at privilege have enabled those

[129]

who lead its forces to combine with the masses to halt the advance of Fascism. So far, in its development, the Fascist leaders have won remarkable victories. In Europe, Great Britain stands alone in continued resistance to their demands.

And if Great Britain is to win, its leaders, clearly enough, have three immense problems before them. They have, in the first place, to endure before an enemy who, for a time, can mobilize greater resources than they. Granted the ability to endure, they have, in the second place, to turn from the defensive to the offensive; they have to bring the prospect of Fascist defeat before a world which, so far, has seen the Fascists only in the role of conquerors. And that the defeat, thirdly, may be both complete and lasting, they have to persuade the victims of Fascism, including the peoples of Germany and Italy themselves, the men whose spirit has been sometimes broken and always battered, into militant resistance to their conquerors. They have to win a war in the course of which they have to provoke a revolution.

But the revolution, the provocation of which is an essential condition of their victory, can be a successful one only if it is set in the context of the emerging possibilities of history. It will not come to fruition if it is sought as no more than the means of preserving British privileges, all of them rooted in an economy that is dying, from the assault of Germans and Italians. More than this: it is reasonable to doubt whether the preservation of British privilege, even if masked more attractively as the defence of capitalist democracy in Great Britain, will prove a sufficient basis for the British endurance that will be required in any long struggle. The Britain that fights the Fascist leaders is an alliance of interests formed for defence after the forces of privilege, up to Narvik in sole charge of running the war, had failed to retain the confidence of the nation. That alliance has still to discover its permanent principles of action. It has still to show that it has the imagination and the courage fully to evoke the dynamic of British democracy.

For, in effect, the purpose of this war is the revolution to which British success will give rise. The power to make it will come in part from the impact of British victories themselves, in part from the hope these victories will arouse in the victims of Fascism. My argument here is the vital one that this power depends on beginning now the transformation of Great Britain into a more equal and more just society, that, as this is accomplished, it at once steels the endurance and resolution of the masses, and, as knowledge of it permeates the countries now under the Fascist yoke, it will light flames there that no terrorism will be able to quench. But the transformation must be big enough in range and depth to

[131]

make it evident that the partnership between privilege and the masses is of a permanent character. It is not enough to make concessions to this group and that which, when the danger of defeat has passed, can be withdrawn on the pretext that economic circumstances do not justify their continuance. The way to victory lies in producing the conviction now among the masses that there are to be no more distressed areas, no more vast armies of unemployed, no more slums, no vast denial of genuine equality of educational opportunity. The resolution of the masses is a function of the power of the British leaders to persuade them that the purpose of the war is in reality the defence of a democracy that will not have to risk its fortunes to privilege when the victory is won. A call to equality of sacrifice must not mean the preservation of privilege in the name of democracy.

Let us be clear that there is this danger. That unity in face of the common enemy so remarkably shown since the Battle of France began still masks the persistence of a good deal of what Prof. Tawney has so well termed our religion of inequality. There has not yet been evident that employment of democratic principle which begins the remaking, in a fundamental way, of the pattern England presents to the outside world. Privilege still obtains preference in appointments. Privilege is still able to organize escape for the children of the comfortable. Even in internment questions, the cloak of privilege has been used to protect aristocratic enemy aliens while humbler but well-tested fighters against Fascism whose nationality is, at the moment, formal have been sent into internment camps. Immense powers have been taken by the government over persons and property, but so far those powers have been exercised rather over persons and their rights than over property. The trade unions cheerfully surrender, knowing full well the risks they run, the economic safeguards they have built up after years of effort; we do not hear of any parallel surrender on the part of the employers. That high dividends continue to be paid, not seldom in the firms connected with the war effort, is evidence of the persistence of that rentier mentality which is of all foes of democracy the most insidious and pertinacious. The inevitable increase in the cost of living has already begun to affect the workers' standard of life; it cannot yet, at any rate, be seriously said that the increase in taxation has seriously affected the pleasant ways of life to which the rich in Great Britain are accustomed. The war has profoundly affected the quality and quantity of the education that is offered to the poor; it has but slightly affected that of the rich.

There have been, it is true, important concessions in social welfare. After a century's striving, the need

[133]

to keep men on the land has resulted in a living wage for the agricultural labourer, though here it is notable that there have been farmers mean enough to seek to recoup themselves by compelling their men to work longer hours and increasing the rents of their cottages. The extension of the range of unemployment insurance, the doubling of old-age pensions, the increase of the allowances to wounded members of the forces or the dependants of those killed, are all of them solid achievements which go deep into the lives of the common people. It is vital not to neglect their significance.

But when all is detached of such measures, the fact remains that no measure has yet been forthcoming from the British government which would have as its consequence any serious change in the distribution of economic power. If the war ended with victory tomorrow, it would find virtually unchanged the relation of privilege to the masses. And this means that all the social problems we confronted on the eve of war would remain unaltered, save that the economic balance-sheet of capitalist democracy would, if the experience of the last war is any guide, toughen and tighten the resistance of the privileged to continuance of a policy of social reform. They would say that the nation could not afford the cost. They would mean that, with victory won, they were not prepared to make the sacrifice.

[134]

What Are We to Do Next?

We should have emerged from the struggle with an unchanged dynamic and with the position of the masses in the strategy of economic power greatly worsened. That way, I believe, lies disaster, since it presages the certainty of a social conflict that will threaten the democratic structure for which we have been fighting.

Mr. Wells has spoken, with his customary vividness, of an eminent churchman who "has transferred all that assertiveness to his property, and more particularly to his investment list. For him, typically, as for vast multitudes of his class, the central sustaining reality in life is neither God nor Church, nor country nor duty, nor any of those brave, decorative things, but the investment list, and the income it yields."[1] The mentality implicit in Mr. Wells's description is far more widespread than we care to admit, and it explains, as no other single cause explains, not only the imperfections of capitalist democracy as we know it, but also that tenderness for Fascism which is a primary cause of our present danger. It is the mentality which welcomed Munich as a great victory, and is above all anxious that the present war should be won with the minimum invasion of existing economic rights. It is the mentality, moreover, which, more than any other single factor, explains the surrender of France; it is this mentality

[1] *The Common Sense of War and Peace*, Penguin, 1940, p. 40.

upon which Pétain and Laval were able to build when they betrayed French democracy.

My point, therefore, is the simple one that if we are to discover the secret of a victory the results of which we are not to throw away we must use the dramatic opportunity of the common danger, the deep sense of unity it enforces upon us all, to break the power of this mentality now. That is the highroad to the discovery of the dynamic of democracy. To break it means that if we win the war with unexpected speed we shall not as last time, lose the peace; while if victory is long in coming, breaking the power of this mentality enormously increases the power of the masses to resist. For it not only allays their fears of the future; it gives them hope in, and exhilaration about, that future. It confirms their faith in our announced national purpose, and there is a strength in that confirmation it is difficult to exaggerate.

I do not propose here to draw up a bill of particulars; that would require a separate treatise for its validation. I am content to argue that it is the part of wisdom to offer proof that this mentality is abdicating by beginning in the midst of war a great programme of social reconstruction. Obviously enough, the pressure of the war effort must make it symbolical rather than conclusive, but we must not forget the degree to which men live by symbols. If the

government, for example, were to take off the Statute
Book the Trade Union Law Amendment Act of
1927, which to the working class is above all the
revenge extracted by this mentality for what to the
workers was the supreme gesture of fraternal solidarity they would have attempted, it is certain that
the psychological results would be impressive. If
the foundations were laid now for great educational
reforms in the immediate aftermath of the war, the
conviction would grow that our religion of inequality
is not a permanent feature of the social landscape.
If to these were added three or four measures which
took vital elements in the economic life of the nation
from the sphere of profit-making, there would be
nothing in the fortunes of war, however long it
lasted, however bitter its vicissitudes, that could
break the determination of the workers to win it.
They could see that "pluto-democracy" saw in its
partnership with the masses the need to recognize
the claims of a new world. They would recognize
the basis of immense experiment capable of being
conducted in terms of reasoned consent. We should
be given—what we shall, above all, require—time to
discover the basis of accommodation upon which to
build our revolution.

And the impact of these measures would com-
municate itself to the world outside. It is difficult to
exaggerate the influence that they would have. It is

not only that thereby we strike the ground from under the feet of our critics; we prove that we have both the courage and the faith in ourselves even in time of war to begin by consent the process of fundamental change in a democratic way. We prove to the victims of Fascist conquest what the implications of our victory mean for the masses amongst them. We give them a cause for which to fight which is rooted in one of the strongest of all human motives, the incentive to action which the hope of improving their condition excites in men. And we must remember that we are appealing for revolt to populations whose parties and trade unions have been suppressed precisely because it was for action based upon that incentive that they were formed. We renew the tradition among the workers both in the Fascist states and in those which the dictators have conquered which, everywhere in the last century, has been the main safeguard of democratic security.

For it is not accident that the main opponents of Fascism everywhere, and the chief victims of its atrocity, have been the working class and its leaders. It was so in Italy and in Germany; it was so in Spain; it was the workers who conducted the heroic defence of Warsaw when the Polish armies were broken and their leaders had fled to safety. We do not find the workers or their leaders among the men who assisted Marshal Pétain to organize the surrender of France, and it is notable that, with ourselves, no body of men has so consistently or so strongly denounced the practices of Fascism as the members of the trade unions. It is they and their sons who form the bulk of our defence-forces; it is their effort in factory and workshop which can alone produce the material basis of victory.

Is it not, therefore, clear that the way to win from these men the endurance and the resolution we require is to show that the purpose of the victory we seek is their purpose? We cannot hope, I suggest, to retain their faith unless we prove to them by action that their spirit and objectives are also the spirit and objectives of the British government. For, after all, the power of any government to make men accept its purposes lies in the works by which it proves the reality of those purposes, and not merely by its reiterated announcement of them. What constitutes the appeal of Mr. Churchill's great pronouncements on the end we have in view is not simply the splendour of their form, but the belief, in those who listen to them, that they really mean the coming of a new day. And if we commence now the preparations for its coming, nothing can prevent the hope and exhilaration they will create among the workers from communicating themselves to the workers beyond

[139]

this island. If we want the winds of democratic doctrine to blow through Europe, we must first set them
in play in Great Britain.

What is the answer to this view? It takes, I think,
two forms, one of principle and one of practice; they
require different treatment. This war, it is said, is a
war for democracy; it is a defence of the procedures
of freedom and popular rule; it is not a defence of
particular economic relationships to which those procedures may, in appropriate political circumstances,
be legitimately devoted. It is unfair and unwise to
use the difficulties created by the war for objects
which, whatever their validity, were repudiated by
the electorate upon the last occasion when it could
be consulted.

This is, I think, a fallacious view. Procedures are
no doubt important in themselves, but they are also
important for what they do and what they make
possible. The democracy we have known in Western
Europe has been everywhere set in the context of
capitalism, and where Fascism has overthrown
democracy it has always been because, within the
framework of democratic procedures, ends were
sought which were deemed incompatible with the
economic system capitalism requires. It is useless to
argue that this cannot happen in Great Britain because with ourselves the democratic tradition is far
more deeply rooted, for it has happened in France,

[140]

where the democratic tradition was at least as profound. To associate the defence of democracy with the defence of the immediate distribution of social power in Great Britain is to take a purely static view of democracy. The truth rather is that political procedures cannot be separated from the ends men seek to make them serve. To argue, therefore, that the objectives of British democracy must be those of the Britain which entered the war is to fail to note that the experience of the war, by its very intensity, changes those objectives. And unless we recognize that the procedures of freedom and popular rule are made valid for those who live by them in terms of their ability to satisfy the demands they encounter, we shall omit to notice that dynamic factor in politics the interpretation of which is the test of statesmanship.

It is, of course, true that the kind of policy I am here advocating was repudiated by the British electorate in 1935. That does not mean that the British government is not entitled to adopt it if, in its judgment and that of Parliament, it is a policy of which the results are desirable. Mr. Chamberlain's foreign policy from 1937 to 1939 was a repudiation of the principles his party put before the electorate in 1935 and approved by it. Mr. Churchill had no sort of electoral authority for a sudden offer of governmental union between Great Britain and France which he offered to the latter just before the final surrender of the Pétain government. Because circumstances change between one general election and another, every British Cabinet is conceded the right, within the limits of prudence, to adapt its policy to new circumstances, provided that it can secure the approval of Parliament for its adaptation; and the final judgment upon its elastic interpretation of its mandate is given by the voters at the next general election. The sole question, therefore, raised by the policy here advocated is whether it can be regarded as within the limits of prudence.

It is then said that such a policy as this would jeopardize the unity of the nation at a time when the preservation of that unity is fundamental to victory. But why should it do this? The only ground upon which it could have that result is that the privileged classes would view its implications as a threat to their privileges. Their enthusiasm for victory would then begin to wane, if the government persisted; alternatively, that persistence would result in its defeat in the House of Commons and its replacement by one which took a more moderate view of the limits of prudence.

Either of these alternatives has implications of the highest importance. If the adoption of such a policy by the British government caused a decline in the enthusiasm of the privileged classes for victory, the

lesson of that decline would obviously be that they
cared more for their privileges than for democratic
procedures; and this would emphasize the point I
have been making that the separation of procedures
from ends is not in fact possible. If, to satisfy the
privileged conception of the prudent, a government
which adopted this policy was defeated in the House
of Commons, it would clearly have to be reconsti-
tuted without labour support. This would go far to
the destruction of national unity, since it would be
an announcement that no policy is admissible during the war which, in the judgment of the privileged
classes, violates their conception of prudence. They
would be claiming, in fact, a veto in wartime upon
the ends to which democratic procedures may be
devoted, at a price which, in the circumstances,
would be certain to outrage organized labour in
Great Britain and to have immense psychological
repercussions abroad. Either alternative would, in
fact, be the repudiation of democracy for privilege.
That would, I think, be merely the first step, though
it would be a big step, toward the possibility of
Fascism in Great Britain.

Capitalist democracy, it may be argued, is at best
a fragile thing; however fragile, what it offers the
masses is infinitely better than anything Fascism
offers them. Is it not, then, the part of wisdom to
concentrate upon policies which unite, rather than

divide, the nation? Much can be done within the traditional routines of concession, which, for the sake of victory, privilege will be glad to give. Indeed, on this plane, it has already given much: unemployment insurance has been vastly extended, the wages of agricultural workers have been greatly increased, old-age pensions have been virtually doubled. If the demands of the workers during the war stay within a realm traced by concessions of this character, there will be no threat to the national unity. We can then postpone until after the war those ultimate questions of economic constitution the mere raising of which sets the signals of democracy at danger.

The simple answer, of course, to this argument is that history has raised those ultimate questions now and, therefore, to face them courageously is part of the necessary strategy of victory. It is obvious, moreover, that the cost of fighting the war will not permit the making of the traditional concessions either on a large scale or in a continuous way; or, if they were made, the level of taxation that would result of itself would be fatal to privilege and, upon the argument, have the same effect as the policy I have urged. But what is further clear is that the defence of traditional concessions as the desirable path of prudence is an index to the temper of privilege which must be underlined. For if it rejects this policy in time of war,

when a common danger drives men to forget their
differences, how much more likely is it to reject it
when victory has been won and the need to win the
support of the masses is so much less intense. At a
time when it asks the working classes to sacrifice a
large part of their traditional mechanisms of economic defence, in effect it refuses to put its own in
jeopardy. It then emerges from the war with its own
defences unbroken, with concessions made that can
easily be withdrawn, on the ground that the nation
must cut its coat according to its cloth (one can
almost hear the sharpening of the Geddes axe), and
with the workers deprived of those regulations by
which in peace they are able to protect their standard of life. To argue that in such a situation the forces
of democracy would meet those of privilege on equal
terms is fantastic. The workers of Great Britain are
patient and generous to a fault; but they are not so
stupid as to surrender their arms before the battle
has been joined. That is the invitation with which
this argument presents them.

The truth is that the price of this war is the making of a more equal society, and the road to it lies
through the ending of those vested interests which
subordinate to profit-making the reconstruction that
price entails. I have already spoken of the evidence
which points clearly to our entrance upon a revolutionary phase of history. We have to adjust the rela-

tions of our society to its claims; all the struggles of the past twenty-five years, with their culmination in the present war, are simply a part of the process of that adjustment. The dictators have sought to arrest its development, at first as the agents of privilege, subsequently for the maintenance of their own personal power. To do so, as I have sought to show, they have been compelled to embark upon a programme of world conquest; they have no other means of satisfying their own peoples. For the alternative they would confront is adjustment to the revolution, and the conditions that adjustment would necessitate would make their habits impossible and their persons superfluous.

My argument is that we are not less involved than the Fascist countries in this revolution; we are fighting them because their rulers seek its arrest at our expense. But even if we win, we have still to come to terms with it. It poses precisely the same problems for us as it has posed for our enemies. We can meet them, if we will, by consent, or we can meet them, as in Italy and Germany, in terms of violent conflict, but we still have to meet them. What I have been urging here is a policy built upon the assumption that to meet these problems by consent is better than to meet them by violence. I have not denied that to do so will require profound adaptations in our society, above all in the habits of those who live by privilege.

But I have argued that war is a condition peculiarly adapted by its nature to enable the process of adaptation by consent to begin. For its scale and its intensity have shaken us all out of our routines. It has created the expectation of experiment. It has aroused a predisposition to novelty. More important, perhaps, even than this is that it has created the psychological conditions in which, under great leadership, men are prepared for great sacrifices. In relatively a small way that will be evident to anyone who compares the national temper, and the effort it has made possible under Mr. Churchill and under Mr. Chamberlain. Even if it be said that part of the change is an awakening to the proximity of external danger, my point remains that great leadership can direct the new spirit to the larger objectives I have stressed. And wisely so directed, it can make those larger objectives a re-enforcement of the strength of the nation in the war.

It can do so because those who adapt the life of a people to the claims of a new order find always that the adaptation invigorates and increases the national power. It was so in the Cromwellian epoch; it was so in the French Revolution; and this same *élan* has been a feature noted by every careful observer of the Russian Revolution. It is able to do so because it taps the immense reservoirs of unused energy and capacity that are unduly confined in any society in which, as in the old Europe from which, though we hardly know it, we are fighting to free ourselves, the political relations are in contradiction with the possibilities of the productive relations. We can see that in a small way by noting that the suspension of those trade-union restrictions which were the workers' reply to the power of capitalist privilege has released productive forces urgent to victory in the war. In the same way, but upon a far larger scale, a similar effect would follow by suspending the vested interests of capitalist privilege. And by such suspension we should have taken a long and important step toward the realization of that potential economy of abundance which science has now brought within our grasp.

We can, I say, capture that *élan* for the purposes of war if we proceed by consent; we shall not capture it otherwise. For if victory comes more shortly than we expect, the problems of adaptation will remain; and, on all the evidence, we shall shrink back into our wonted habits without the chance that the psychological compulsions of war impose to make the effort toward consent when, relatively, it can be made with ease. And, if the war be prolonged, fatigue and want and disillusion, and the suffering these cause, will, in the absence of adaptation, strain our power to maintain unity if not to the breaking-point, as in France, certainly to the point at which conflict will come after the war. The dilemma that conflict will then pose to us is the dilemma which Germany and Italy resolved by choosing Fascism and the consequences involved in that choice.

We have at least the supreme good fortune to have been warned, as it were, by history of the results of the choice before us. Fascism is the epitaph upon those forces of privilege which seek to imprison the future by defending with violence an obsolete past. The same epitaph will be applicable to ourselves if we follow that path, because the same forces are at work, even if with retardation, among ourselves. For we must never forget that at once the policy of our rulers in the period of appeasement and the habits of those who saw in the outlaws men who might give them, too, release from the implications of the democratic way of life are massive evidence of how nearly we were driven into collaboration with them for the sake of privilege. It is curious, but true, that in the disaster of war we have been given another chance to choose wisely. The central issue before us is whether we take that chance.

It is the central issue, and it is difficult to emphasize too strongly how profoundly it is the central issue. For what Great Britain does in this epoch of the world's refashioning sets the habit of the rest of the world. If we go forward, we give, more fully than ever before, its letters of credit to democracy. We

[149]

assure the break-up of the dictators' power to hold down their own peoples and the conquests these have been driven by them to make. We find, that is to say, the one effective formula for their liberation: the appeal to the revolutionary consciousness of the masses to become the masters of their own destiny. And if it be said that this is an appeal to the masses to overthrow the forces of privilege in the dictatorial and occupied countries, the answer is the final one, first, that it is those forces which brought the outlaws to power, and, second, it is they, also, which have collaborated with them, as in France, to use defeat for the overthrow of democracy. Victory means their destruction, and the one sure way to destroy them is to call to revolt, and thence to power, the men who have no hope save as we are able to restore and consolidate democratic institutions.

One other point in this context I must make. I have discussed the reasons, so disappointing to ourselves, which led the Soviet Union not only to assume a position of armed neutrality in this conflict—a grim repudiation of her former leadership in the fight against the Fascist outlaws—but which led her leaders to assume that it was a matter of indifference to her interests whether Fascism or capitalist democracy was victorious. My analysis of the nature of Fascism has sought to provide grounds for the view that this attitude of indifference was a short-sighted policy; a Fascist victory makes the Soviet Union an inevitable objective of Fascist attack. And even if that attack could be held, the price that the Soviet Union would have to pay for it would postpone for decades her ability to reap the fruits of her immense social experiment. For she would have to divert to militarization the production of consumption goods on a scale far beyond any her armed neutrality requires. And since it is pretty obvious that a serious attack from the Fascist West would be paralleled by one from the Fascist East, the danger this implies to the Soviet Union requires no elaboration.

Now this is a danger that is removed by the defeat of the Fascist West. But the goodwill of the Soviet Union depends upon our ability to produce the conviction in her rulers that this defeat is, in sober fact, a defeat of those forces which, ever since 1917, have threatened her security: the conviction, that is, that the defeat of Western Fascism is the victory of Western democracy. The rulers of the Soviet Union are obviously not convinced that the one is the other. They are not convinced of this for the good reason that the civil wars and the intervention were at every turn dependent upon the support of the Western democracies or, rather, of the forces of privilege within them. The best way of convincing the Soviet Union that this danger cannot recur is to prove that these forces will not again be either able or willing

to threaten its security, and the best way to produce
that conviction is to begin the process in the Western democracies of ending the power of privilege to
think in these terms. If it is said that such a fear is
unfounded, the answer, I think, is the very important one that Soviet policy all over the world, as is
shown by the attitude of Communist Parties in Great
Britain, France, and the United States in particular,
is built, however mistakenly, upon that assumption.
This is shown, above all, in the incredible tergiversa-
tions of the British Communist Party. It began the
war by taking the view, inherent in the very essence
of its doctrine, that the defeat of Fascism was vital
to the interest of the workers. In just over a month
it was insisting that this was an imperialist war, the
termination of which, on almost any terms, was desirable. Since then, with a variety of emphasis, though
it has insisted that Fascism is evil, it has mostly continued to deny that this is fundamentally an anti-
Fascist war. Upon this assumption it has used all its
energies to divide and limit working-class support
for the war. The tragic results of the view it has
taken are best evident in the fate of France and the
destruction there of that Communist leadership
which, under other circumstances, had a great role
to play in organizing resistance to the Fascism of the
Pétain-Laval government.

It is an obvious temptation, especially to those

whose politics is of the Left, to dismiss the Communist tactic as unimportant, especially because the numerical support it commands is small. But there are several reasons why, in my own judgment, this is a completely mistaken view. In the first place, it reflects directly the Soviet Union's conviction that, in the last resort, the destruction of the Russian experiment is not less the purpose of capitalist democracy than of Fascism; and there is real need, in the light of history, for assurance that this is not so. It is notable, for example, that hardly any action of the war called forth such enthusiasm from the defenders of capitalist privilege as the opportunity the Soviet attack—a blunder of the first magnitude—upon Finland seemed to give for the long-sought revenge for the Revolution of 1917. It is particularly notable, to take an example from a non-belligerent power, that ex-President Hoover, who had evinced not a particle of interest in the Fascist attack on Republican Spain, was in the front rank of those Americans who urged every possible assistance for Finland, and that he had, during the four years of his Presidency, consistently denied diplomatic recognition to the Soviet Union. It is notable, in Great Britain, that one of the most outstanding advocates of military assistance to Finland was Lord Phillimore, who had been also one of the most outstanding advocates of a Franco victory for Spain. The Communist inference that the enemies of the Soviet Union still sought eagerly for the chance to organize its destruction is not, in the light of the facts, unintelligible.

And it must be remembered, further, that the whole Communist approach to capitalist democracy is based upon an estimate of the balance of forces it represents which assumes, first, that capitalist power is immensely stronger than democratic power and, second, that this capitalist power will not surrender its privileges without fighting for them. I hardly need, in the light of Fascist history, to summarize the massive body of evidence, so grimly supplemented by the recent experience of France, which supports this view. The real answer to it lies not in a counter-estimate which stresses the deep roots of the democratic tradition in Great Britain and the United States, but in the proof by actual deeds that, to win a democratic victory, capitalist power has actually begun to strip itself of its privileges. For, otherwise, on his assumptions, with the weight behind them of the events through which we have passed, the Communist is entitled to reply that, as soon as victory has been won, capitalist privilege will throw off the mask and repudiate the alliance it has made with the workers because its interests are once more safe.

To this must be added one further argument of considerable psychological importance. "There is a new government," the Communist emphasizes, "and,

no doubt, labour leaders have places of importance
in its ranks. But, predominantly, it is still the government which pursued the policy of appeasement,
truckled at every turn, to Mussolini yesterday, as it
truckles to Franco Spain and Japan today, the government, moreover, which refused to call upon the
people to make the effort proportionate to victory
because it was not prepared to ask for parallel sacrifices from the forces of privilege." To the Communist,
in short, the Churchill government is largely the old
firm under a new name. Its tactic is an invitation to
the labour and trade-union leaders to mobilize the
energy of the workers for a victory of privilege; if
they will be able to secure some minor concessions
in return for their contribution, they will not be able
to exact that revolution by consent which alone gives
meaning to the workers' effort, and their support will
be repudiated once the help of the workers has served
the capitalist turn. This after all, they say, is the con-
sistent history of capitalist democracy. It is what occurred in the Cromwellian wars; that is the meaning
of the movements headed by Lilburne and Winstan-
ley. It is what occurred in the French Revolution;
that explains the suppression of the *Enragés* and the
execution of Babeuf. It is what happened, once more,
in 1848; Louis Napoleon was used by property to act
as the executioner of working-class aspirations much
in the manner in which Hitler was used by big busi-

ness in Germany. It is what would have happened, finally, under Kerensky in the Soviet Union, had not Lenin led the working-class forces to victory there.

Nothing at all is gained, I believe, by denying the power of this argument. It may be easy to show that in each past instance of deception the forces of the working class were too weak and too unorganized to permit the aspirations of their leaders to take an effective place in history, and it may be easy to show, too, that in each past instance the power of capitalism to expand enabled it to offer concessions to the masses of a character which went far to compensate for the deception and, pretty clearly, satisfied their demands.

But that power of capitalism, as a universal system, to expand has now clearly reached its term. That is why this war has come upon us. That is why it is the strategy of the Fascist leaders to win opportunities for one national capitalism at the expense of another; why, after victory, its effort to stabilize power consists in the reduction of those whom it conquers to slavery. The dynamic of victory, therefore, consists in breaking those vested interests which stand in the way of the release of those new potentialities of production which are at our disposal. And the way, once more, to prove that the Communist diagnosis is wrong is for the British government to initiate of its own volition the break-up of those interests. By so doing, and only by so doing, it shows that it has really grasped the nature of this war. By refusing to do so, it merely postpones internal conflict to a later stage. For, if the causes which produced this war are to be seriously tackled, we have to take the chance that is offered us now of replacing the foundations of an economics of scarcity by those adapted to an economics of abundance.

The policy I have advocated here begins that task of replacement, and the wisdom of our leadership is tested by its capacity to see its implications in time. Totalitarian war makes so profound an impact upon the economy of a people that it necessarily drives our statesmen back to the foundations of the state. It is of course true, as Edmund Burke said, that it is always dangerous to meddle with foundations; the answer, equally of course, is that the situation leaves us no alternative. Our problem is whether the past habits of those among our leaders who control the majority in Parliament are so compelling that they will not be able objectively to measure the volume of adaptation that is required. It is here, obviously, that the task of the labour leaders in the government is at once so urgent and so delicate. They know the necessity of this adaptation. It is the central principle of their doctrine; it is, above all, for its realization that they were sent into the government. They can work there in an atmosphere more persuasive than at any other time for that realization.

[157]

For they know that the will of the nation is united to secure victory; they know, also, that without this adaptation victory is, at best, uncertain and, at the worst, may, even when achieved, be merely, without it, a postponement of the problems that the acceptance of its necessity would go far to solve. They know, too, that the mind of the nation is prepared for great changes, and that the very drama of their preparation induces a mood of exhilaration—the historic temper of all popular revolutions—and steels the resolution the will to victory requires. They know, too, that victory cannot be won without their support, since its withdrawal would strike a fatal blow at the unity upon which it has to be built. Given efficiency and goodwill they need to demand neither proscription of persons nor expropriation of property. They need only to insist, as the price of their support, upon the necessity for this government of using the procedures of democracy to inaugurate the process of adaptation its victory requires. No doubt that insistence will demand from them the exercise of all their determination of heart and persuasiveness of intelligence. No doubt, also, they will find the process of securing conviction of the necessity a series of sudden decisions rather than an unwavering straight line. But behind them is not only the full strength of the organized movement they represent. Behind them, also, there is a large body of inde-

[158]

pendent support, not committed to any tightness of
doctrine, but ready, even eager, to throw its whole
weight behind whatever principles of action increase
the prospects of victory. It is an immense responsibility, but it is also an opportunity proportionate to
the responsibility. Not to take it, as the tide flows to
flood-level, would be a betrayal, on their part, of one
of the supreme occasions of history. It is, indeed, the
kind of moment that Lenin knew in the Russian Revolution when he called upon his comrades to inaugurate the new social order. It was the condition of his
success that the purpose for which he stood should
depend upon violence for its attainment. It is the
more fortunate opportunity of our leaders that they
have the hope of building the achievement of the
great purpose to which they are called upon the consent of all among their countrymen who have grasped
the conditions of victory. Their task is to make hope
fulfilment.

II

The policy I have been analysing demands the
eager collaboration of free men. They have to bring
to its service all the energy of their minds and hearts,
to harness to its elaboration all the resources, within
our present system so largely unexplored, that science
has placed at our disposal. For, obviously enough, in
a score of vital directions the possibilities of scientific

[159]

discovery are ignored, and half the circumstances of their neglect will be found, on examination, to lie in the opposition to their exploitation of some vested interest of privilege. That is so not merely in the immediate situation, our failure, for instance, to adapt, by proper scientific experiment, the Spanish experience of anti-tank measures to the defence against German tactics in the Battle of France,[2] or in our failure to relate the problems of camouflage to their bases in biology and psychology.[3] It is even more evident in such long-term problems as the food-supply, the generation and distribution of electric power, the design, from the angle both of industrial efficiency and of the workers' health, of factories and workshops, the proper use of psychology in the art of industrial management. In all these realms, to take examples only, the prospects of science limp behind their dependence upon the requirements of the profit-making motive. Its possibilities are sacrificed to the mentality of that rentier outlook Mr. Wells has so admirably described.

It is the knowledge that this sacrifice is inherent in the present social order which has led Mr. Wells, and a body of devoted collaborators, to publish a "Declaration of the Rights of Man" and to demand

[2] See an interesting comment upon this in *Science in War*, Penguin, 1940, pp. 35 ff.

[3] See an interesting comment upon this in *Science in War*, Penguin, 1940, pp. 42 ff.

its inclusion in the peace aims of the democracies. I have no quarrel with the declaration; each of its terms seems to me an essential protection of freedom and therefore an essential part of any effective democratic procedure. Without the enjoyment of the rights Mr. Wells and his colleagues prescribe, there can be no doubt at all, in the light of historical experience, that no class of men is free which has only its labour-power to sell. And this is to say that no state in which such a class of men exists can in any real sense be a democracy.

But Mr. Wells would be the first to agree that a declaration of rights is not the same thing as its realization; the problem is to bridge the gap between promise and fulfilment. Declarations of rights are not new in history; neither, even, are the announcements of devices whereby they may be put beyond the reach of invasion. Few American states but have them in profusion; few but have seen them ruthlessly thrown overboard by relentless men with whose privileges they interfered. The Weimar Constitution offered to German citizens a body of rights almost as wide as those demanded by Mr. Wells; the history of the Weimar Republic is the record of their uneasy shrinkage into nothing. The Soviet Constitution of 1936 gave to Soviet citizens a complex of guarantees even wider than those of Weimar; the suspicion of danger latent in them to the present holders of power has meant that thus far they have remained an empty declaration without due substance in the lives of men.

I do not mean to imply that declarations of this kind are valueless; on the contrary. It is always a useful thing to attach a solemn significance to the fundamental and tested procedures of freedom if only that their violation may evoke protest and, if possible, resistance; for in the last resort the courage to resist is the permanent secret of freedom. My point is rather that acceptance of the procedures waxes and wanes in terms of the security men feel about the foundations of the social order; and that security, in its turn, is a function of the capacity for economic expansion of that social order. As soon as that capacity is in danger, men spring to the defence of their wonted way of life, and if the procedures of freedom jeopardize that way, then they are thrown overboard. This is why war and revolution are so frequently the parent of dictatorship; each represents the threat of danger to an interest deemed more important by those who share in its benefits than the procedure of freedom which might entitle their opponents to question the validity of the interest involved.

If freedom, then, is a function of security, the rights it will be able to protect will be proportionate, both in volume and intensity, to the degree of security

[162]

that is attained. Their total denial, for example, in the Fascist system is essentially a measure of the insecurity their rulers feel about their ability to maintain their power; the massive exclusion from the enjoyment of rights they have organized indicates their fears for their future. But, with appropriate changes of emphasis, the same conclusion applies to Great Britain. Even if its rulers adopted Mr. Wells's "Declaration of Rights," it would remain no more than a propagandist gesture unless the social order was organized that is capable of supporting it. And that social order cannot be organized without the revolution of which I have spoken.

For without it there will not be the resources available to satisfy the demands of the masses; and because those demands cannot be satisfied, victory or no victory, the forces of privilege will then continuously feel that their interests are insecure. They are then bound to do all they can to protect them from attack, and they will take the obvious road, always taken in these conditions, of stultifying the declaration of rights. They may not even overtly admit its stultification; they may well rely, as in the United States in the period of the "Red hysteria" during 1919–20, upon that technique of distinguishing between "liberty" and "licence" which enables them to salve their consciences while opposing their opponents. But in the end the result will be the same as its open destruction, unless there supervenes that era of economic expansion which makes them convinced that they can with safety make concessions to the demands they encounter.

In any period, this is to say, where men differ profoundly upon matters of social constitution the procedures of democracy are at a discount until a new equilibrium of agreement has been found. If it cannot be found by consent, it must be imposed by force; in the latter event it must obviously contradict the vital implications of a democratic scheme. It is no use to rely, as I think Mr. Wells relies, upon the inherent intellectual validity of such a declaration as he has preferred for its acceptance. If reason always prevailed over unreason, the outlaws would not now be in power in the Fascist states. The fact is that whenever privilege, above all privilege connected with the relations of property, is in danger it flies into that panic which is the mortal enemy of reason; and it is a waste of time to ask its consideration of arguments that, in another mental climate, it is capable of understanding.

That is why our opportunity at this moment to begin our revolution by consent is so unique. The interests of privilege are threatened on two fronts. On the one side, the Fascist leaders threaten the annihilation of the British Empire; on the other, the masses ask for a beginning to be made of a funda-

mental redistribution of economic power. I am arguing here that the repulse of the first threat means
finding terms of peace with the second. For if the
Fascist leaders were to succeed, the position of those
whom they have conquered shows that the privilege
they would leave could reach but a little way, and
the very fact that it existed under their patronage
would be a constant threat to its security. And even
if the threat of annihilation were repulsed without
the redistribution I have urged as necessary, it would
still leave the forces of privilege face to face with its
claims; the insecurity would continue until they were
either satisfied or suppressed.

It is therefore, as I conceive, the part of wisdom
to satisfy them; to reform, if you would preserve, is
as Macaulay said of the Reform Bill of a century ago,
"the watchword of great events." To co-operate with
the masses in beginning now the revolution that has
become necessary has immense advantages. It
strengthens our power to wage the war. It gives us
the best assurance available that the mood of resistance to Hitler abroad will be prepared and adequate when the time comes for its effective evocation.
It mitigates the suspicions of our purposes that have
so unnecessarily thrown away the support that was
available from the Soviet Union.

These are, as I say, immense advantages; but they
do not exhaust the possibilities of this policy. Not the

least of the benefits it offers us is the chance it gives of gaining time. It permits, by the evolutionary basis on which it is built, the forces of privilege to prepare themselves for, and adapt themselves to, the idea of fundamental change; and it persuades the workers to recognize that there is not the danger of resistance to that idea. I do not, of course, deny that it exacts from the privileged more than they would wish to give, as, certainly, it yields to the workers far less than they wish to take. The simple answer is that, like all processes of consent, it is a compromise; and compromise of this character lies at the heart of successful democracy. And it must be remembered, at every moment of its consideration, first, that what it exacts from the privileged is far less than the outlaws would demand and, second, that it offers the prospect, if it emerges as a compromise made with good-will, of a security that cannot be had on other conditions. For I repeat that without this experiment the objective historical circumstances in which we live make violent readjustment certain. We can escape its consequences only by welcoming the implications of democracy. With an experiment of this kind, we can adapt our society peacefully to the demands of the future. Without it, whatever the rhetoric in which our announced purposes be absorbed, we shall merely move forward here to a repetition of the tragedy out of which, elsewhere, this war has emerged.

We fight to preserve democracy and freedom. We have, therefore, to conquer in our own society those inherent tendencies of privilege to deny to democracy and freedom any power to expand which threatens its vested interests. We have to conquer them, as I have argued, as the very condition of the victory we seek. I do not say we shall conquer them. I only say that, if we should will to do so, we have the power and that, without that will, a fate akin to that of France is certain to be ours. History could have given us no ampler warning of the nature of the choice we confront.

But the preservation of democracy and freedom is not, of course, a matter which concerns ourselves alone. As the condition of their safety we have to effect the defeat of the outlaws wherever they have raised their head. Our war is not a struggle of which we can ignore the interconnexions. We who have seen how Japanese success in Manchuria can lead to Italian conquests in Africa and how the German conquest of France may profoundly affect the balance of power in the Far East can see at once that this is an international civil war in which we are engaged. The cleansing of our democracy, this is to say, is a matter of international consequence. We make our aims in this struggle known at least as much by what we do as by what we say. Our friends, not less our enemies, deduce our motives as much from the policy for which we are responsible as from the explanations we issue of its meaning. The enemies of the outlaws should not need to be taught that words are counters, when they are separated from the appropriate deed, with which to twist and corrupt the hearts of men.

This has an obvious bearing upon two phases of our international policy. It influences, first, our position as an empire and the impact of its internal relations upon the outside world, and it influences, secondly, our authority to persuade the peoples of the European Continent, not least the people of Germany, that we genuinely seek a world peace which definitely rules out the possibility of resuming war. I must now analyse the implications of each of these phases.

The first is a complicated one, because the relations of empire are complicated. It touches not only trade and population and access to raw materials, and the important but too neglected opportunity afforded by empire to offer the opportunities of a successful career to several thousands of young men each year; it touches, I may add, each of these more profoundly as, with the decline of capitalist expansion, we are tempted, as at Ottawa, to restrict access to the fruits of empire to less favoured powers. This is part of the general problem of the contradiction between political relations and economic forces which is set up by the collapse of the economic foundations of our civilization.

I select out of this complexity one illustration of the problem of empire, and that the most pivotal of all: India. We have an immense stake in India; without the immense wealth its possession has brought us we should not have been able to meet, at least peacefully meet, the demands of the proletariat in this country. We have, I do not doubt, done much for India that is for its benefit; above all, I think, we have brought it to consciousness of its destiny as a nation. India stands before us today demanding the right to self-government as clearly as ever America or Ireland did, demanding freedom from our paramount power as unmistakably as Poland or Czechoslovakia demands freedom from the paramount power of Germany over them. There is not one popular leader in India, with a serious following behind him, to whom we can appeal for support of the continuance of our paramountcy. Year by year, to maintain it, even in the revised form of 1936, we have to resort to special powers, the exercise of undemocratic authority, the wide use of the power to imprison and to flog. The few Indians of position we can produce to applaud our rule are men whom we have elevated for that purpose, who, without that elevation, as both we and India know, would be against us and not for us. The

main interest we support in India, apart from our own
financial interest, is a mass of feudal princes of whom,
with not more than six exceptions, it can, so far as
the last half-century is concerned, be said with literal
accuracy that the character of their governance com-
petes, in barbarism and squalor, with that of the outlaws in Europe.

The character of our rule in India, maintained in
defiance of Indian demands, has all over the world
long stained our reputation for plain dealing; until
the advent of Hitler and Mussolini, it was the classic
example of imperialist exploitation. We are squarely
faced from India with a demand, insistently maintained, for self-government, and we know within ourselves that sooner or later we must yield to it, even
though the risk to our interests of so yielding is a
formidable one. But we cling to the maintenance of
that interest by every pretext and device we can
discover. The very statesmen who manipulate these
pretexts and devices are most prolific in the announcement of their yearning for the fulfilment of
India's ambition; Sir Samuel Hoare was even shameless enough to represent the Act of 1935, which in-
geniously multiplied every protective device discov-
erable of reaction, as a long step on the road to that
fulfilment. We announce that we shall put no ob-
stacle in the way of Indian freedom; we ask only
that all Indians of every sort shall first agree upon

its pattern. And since that agreement is not forthcoming, we continue to govern India for our own
purposes. Meanwhile, in the name of the Indian people, we ourselves take this and that decision on its
behalf and then proudly thank India for its generosity to us, or we accept this gift or that from one
or other of the Indian princes—their method of in-
suring their further protection from us—which we
know is a gift mostly wrung from the misery of their
unhappy subjects, and then exhibit these gifts as the
proof of Indian "loyalty." I do not know how far we
deceive ourselves by this technique; empire possesses
a large capacity for self-deception. I do know that
we deceive no people beyond the boundaries of our
empire—least of all the Indian people themselves.

It seems to me clear that the solution of the Indian
problem—which is not a simple one on any showing
—depends upon the reality of our determination to
agree to its self-government. If we said, for example,
that this self-government will begin to operate within
a year of the conclusion of peace; if we proposed to
India a constituent assembly elected from the present provincial assemblies and announced, subject to
suitable negotiations with ourselves, that we should
ask Parliament to ratify the conclusions it reached;
if we built a National Government of Indians at
Delhi to conduct the war and the negotiations with
us; if we suggested that such communal differences

[171]

as the assembly failed to solve should be submitted
to independent arbitration, to the Permanent International Court, for instance, or to the President of
the United States; I do not think an appropriate
pattern of Indian freedom would be long in forthcoming. But so long as every vested interest in India
is, like the Moslem interest, encouraged, openly or
secretly, to believe that it will get better terms from
dependence upon us than from a real attempt at accommodation with other Indian interests, of course
agreement between them is not forthcoming. We
patronize these dissidents from unity in the same
way, though much more subtly, as the Conservative
Party has so long patronized the separation of Ul-
ster, and with the same evil consequences.

For the gains that would be available to us from a
free India, bound to us, like the Dominions, by no ties
other than its own choice, would be immense from
any point of view. It is not only, as we have been
made aware, that such an India, even in the stage of
its approach to freedom, would give us a wealth of
aid in the war effort that we cannot dare, under
present conditions, to exact from her. It is not only
that such an India would free us from necessities of
coercion which, when they issue in events like Am-
ritsar, bedevil our domestic politics. It is not only, further, that a free India could begin that fuller exploitation of its own resources which its present service to

[172]

our vested interests at so many points restricts and constrains. It is also that, freeing India now, we remove from the post-war years a problem that will, because it will grow in intensity, hamper by the attention for which it will call our capacity to deal with our own immense issues of reconstruction. It is, above all, because the recognition by us of India's right to freedom is the supreme announcement we can make to the world that we have done, once and for all, with the older imperialism.

I do not think it is possible to exaggerate the importance of such an announcement, not least in its influence upon the subject peoples of Germany and Italy in whom we are so greatly concerned both to arouse and to sustain hope. We cannot easily exaggerate its beneficent influence upon the Soviet Union or upon liberal opinion in the United States. But every day that we postpone its coming, we diminish the importance it will have. I take this view upon the ground that no policy is more unwise than that which concedes in a period of difficulty a demand which should justly be conceded in a period of ease. The case against that unwisdom was stated, in terms no one can better, by Macaulay nearly a century ago in the very analogous issue of Ireland. "You will make it," he told the House of Commons about the concession of a grant to Maynooth,[4] "as every conces-

[4] *Speeches*, World's Classics ed., p. 276.

sion to Ireland has been made. You will make it when
its effect will be, not to appease, but to stimulate
agitation. You will make it when it will be regarded,
not as a great act of national justice, but as a confession of national weakness. You will make it in such
a way, and at such a time, that there will be but too
much reason to doubt whether more mischief has
been done by your long refusal, or by your tardy and
enforced compliance."

The point I am making is the simple one that
empire is a handicap to freedom whenever its subjects deny the validity of its maintenance. At that
stage it must either become a partnership or de-
generate into a tyranny. And it is particularly dangerous to permit that degeneration when it offers to our
enemies an opportunity of reproach to which we have
no adequate response. The plea made by our enemies
that the real nature of our dominion is shown by the
way in which we maintain our rule in India we cannot answer by reference to a single Indian representative able freely to secure the full support of his own
people. We can answer that plea only by saying that
we are satisfied with our achievement there. But we
have, in truth, no more right to constitute ourselves
judges in our own cause than the Fascist leaders possess; less even, since we deny them that right so soon
as its attempted application touches ourselves. A
nation can justly stand as trustee of another people

when it can be shown that no vested interest of its own is safeguarded by that trusteeship, and when a detached observer would admit, first, that the people so ruled do not claim freedom from trusteeship and, second, when the objective results of its exercise are clearly and mainly for the benefit of that people. Judged by these standards, it is clear, I think, that the sooner we end our paramountcy over India the better for Indians and for ourselves. And there is no moment more fitting to end it than in a war where we declare ourselves to be the world defenders of democracy and freedom. In the long run, it is evident, the interests we maintain by its suppression abroad are interests whose claims we shall regard as paramount also at home. In the infection that attitude compels there lies the grave danger that we shall destroy the end it is our ambition to serve.

IV

At the stage where the organization of our resources permits us to take the offensive, we have to set about the task, on any scrutiny a hard one, of organizing revolt in Germany and Italy and in the territories they have conquered. But we must be clear what we mean by organizing revolt. We seek the overthrow of the outlaws. To overthrow them is both a negative and a positive task. It is negative in the sense that it involves showing the peoples whom they control that the outlaws cannot win. To demonstrate this is, clearly, to destroy the psychological power they derive from the victories they have won. But it still leaves undetermined the vital question of who is to replace them, and that is only another way of asking for whom the victory over them is to be won.

Now if I am right in my assumption that the British government aims, as quite certainly the British people desires, at a permanent peace, the answer to this question can only be that those for whom victory is to be won are the masses. For in a fundamental sense, it is they who lose most by war; in a fundamental sense, also, it is they who lose most when the outlaws obtain power. It is the masses, also, in every country who have fought with the greatest determination both to prevent the coming of the outlaws to power and to undermine them after they have attained it. Not only is this true. It is also of vital importance in this context that the main sources both of defeatism and of betrayal in the countries occupied by Fascism have been the vested interests there. To replace the outlaws by representatives of the vested interests, whether they be generals or aristocrats or big business men, does not solve the issue of enduring peace. It leaves in authority those who connived at the conquests of Fascism. It leaves in being those economic and social conditions which, in the epoch of capitalism in decay, provide the soil in which Fascism grows. It leaves privilege, to put it shortly, in power; and to leave privilege in power is to prohibit exactly that translation from the economics of scarcity to the economics of abundance which alone can give creative meaning to victory.

Let me put this in a very simple way. We shall not reconstitute a Poland which can pursue effectively the policy of the good neighbour merely by replacing the German army of occupation with the successors of Becks and Ridz-Smiglys, with Sapiehas and Lubomirskis; the interests they represented compelled the failure they symbolized. We shall not rebuild France with the Daladiers and the Chautemps, let alone the Pétains and the Lavals. We have to redistribute the whole social and economic power in the conquered countries, because only that redistribution makes possible the basis for an effective reorganization of international relations. Otherwise, obviously, the new vested interests which replace the old will require the retention, for reasons I have already given, of national sovereignty in order to protect their privileges. They will then require military power in order to give meaning to their national sovereignty. The old, and evil, game of power-politics will begin all over again; and quite decisively the consequence of power-politics is war.

It is therefore no good for us simply to state that

our end is victory, or that we fight for liberty and democracy against an evil tyranny which destroys these things. We fight for them, I do not doubt, for ourselves; but we are part of an interdependent world to which we have to prove that in fighting for our liberty and our democracy, we are fighting for theirs too. And to prove it, it is not enough merely to emphasize the immense evils of which the outlaws are guilty. It is not enough to promise them that when the Hitlers and the Mussolinis have gone the Daladiers and the Becks will return. That is merely asking them to replace the major authors of their sufferings by their minor authors. It is not to offer them a cause which has in it the call to an unbreakable resolution. Anyone who knows the position before 1939 of the factory workers or the peasants in Poland under their old masters can see, I think, without difficulty that such a policy would certainly deceive us and in the long run merely betray those to whom it was applied.

We need, this is to say, a strategy of victory which has the right confidently to prophesy social renovation, and that means a strategy which deliberately and consciously plans to end those vested interests which are inherently the enemies of democratic institutions, which have proved themselves so to be in Germany and Italy, in Poland and France, to take only the major instances. But the first way to prove that we have adopted this strategy sincerely is to

[178]

apply it to ourselves. This means, as I have argued, at least the beginning of large-scale social and economic adjustment in Great Britain, and that kind of transformation of our own imperialism which is symbolized by our recognition, in more than verbal fact, of the right of India to self-government. In war, as in equity, it is vital for those who seek justice to come into court with clean hands.

I am confident that, in organizing the strategy of victory, this would be an immense step toward our goal. But it is not enough, and we have to make up our minds that it is not enough. We are dealing with peoples between the devil of one deep fear and the deep sea of another. We urge the German and Italian peoples to throw off the outlaws' yoke; defeat of their empires is the preliminary to that overthrow. But they fear, and in the light of the years since Versailles they are bound to fear, the price of the overthrow to which we urge them. They hear, on all sides, of plans for their forcible subjugation; Germany, for example, is to be repartitioned into that confused medley of petty states from which its unity emerged so painfully in the nineteenth century. Vast reparations are to be exacted from its people to restore the states its enemies have so ruthlessly pillaged and destroyed. This or that territory is to be taken forcibly from her as a strategic safeguard against the recurrence of her febrile nationalism.

In the end, millions of decent, peace-minded Germans must be left with the conviction that their defeat would leave them even worse off and in a more humiliating condition than they are under Hitler. Nor is the atmosphere improved when angry publicists are ready to do what Edmund Burke did not even dare to attempt—draw up a criminal indictment against a whole people.

In the light of the years since 1918, we need, I am confident, to convey three assurances to the German people with all the solemnity of which we are capable. We have to assure them, and the Italian people also, that it will be a peace of genuine negotiation and not a Carthaginian peace. We have to convince them that we do not intend the imposition of either punitive annexations or punitive indemnities. We have to convince them, also, that we shall not, by separating them piecemeal, make their history in the next fifty years a desperate struggle to regain, in the face of our fears of its outcome, the unity they will then have lost. So long as they are unpersuaded of these things, even the Germans and Italians most eager for the defeat of the outlaws are bound to look into the future with grave apprehension, and that is not a mood which provides the effective basis for revolt. For revolt, it cannot be too strongly stressed, comes when men have the hope of genuine liberation, not when they fear that they are to exchange one set of chains for another.

And if we ought to have learned anything from the Peace of Versailles, it is the lesson that a dictated peace, by the mere fact that it is dictated, carries no moral authority for the nations upon whom it is imposed. Even if, as with Versailles, many of its provisions are admirable, it represents a frustration of that national self-respect which, ever since the first partition of Poland, has been a fundamental factor in the modern world. From the other angle, all of us can see this at once if we think of the sense of outrage we had at the terms imposed by Hitler on Czechoslovakia in March 1939, by Mussolini on Abyssinia, or by the Soviet Union on Finland. We have to build our settlement on the maximum of consent and the minimum of coercion. We have to make our enemies feel that they are sharing in the construction of right, not that they are victims of the imposition of what, just because it is imposed, they are certain to regard as wrong.

But all this, important though it is, is yet subordinate to the pivotal condition of enduring peace. That condition is a principle central to the historic constitutional experience of the British people, and it is one, therefore, the world implications of which they should be able to understand as none other. It is simple in its essence, even if, especially in a critical time like ours, it is inevitably complex

[181]

in application: the principle that what touches all must be decided by all.

In a groping and confused way, its significance was recognized at the close of the war of 1914 by those who built the League of Nations. More articulately, it has been grasped by the many makers of schemes of federal union since the nightmare of war descended upon Europe. I do not seek to belittle for one moment the value of these schemes[5]; if they serve only the purpose of persuading public opinion to recognize the obsolescence and therefore the danger of a world divided into national states each fiercely contending for its rights as a sovereign power, they will have done much good. But even the most practical of them, in my opinion, suffers from a fatal defect. They seek to pool sovereignties without attempting to grapple with the vested interests within each state which have so far, because they have been left unmolested, prevented the pooling of sovereignties. They recognize that the flaw in the Covenant of the League of Nations was its admission that the state must remain sovereign. But they proceed to assume—the old fallacy of intellectualism—that, because this was so, states will be prepared simply to abdicate from their sovereignty

[5] The best of them, I think, is that of Dr. W. I. Jennings, *A Federation for Western Europe* (Cambridge, 1940), which has the great merits of clarity and precision. But I think it is open to the criticisms I have discussed in the text.

without dealing with those internal vested interests which compel them to insist upon its retention. They forget the lesson of the British Empire, which, despite long years of effort, has been unable to devise a federal constitution for itself, which, indeed, would within the framework of its present distribution of economic power almost certainly break asunder if the attempt were made. They forget, also, that when the economic interests of the American Union diverged, it took four years of civil war to establish its indissolubility, and that, once again in our own day, the political implications of federalism contradict the economic needs of the United States. The vested interests of America, in the age of giant capitalism, make the states of the Union the reserve-power of reaction.[6]

The will to end sovereignty is, apart from the deliberate organization of the conditions which make its ending possible, as abstract and unreal as a will to justice when those who are so to will are not united by an equal interest in the result of willing. Granted the unequal economic development of European countries in capital accumulation, in power to develop their own resources, in the possession of essential raw materials, and so on, the maintenance

[6] On the causes of the Civil War, by far the best brief treatment is in Louis Hacker, *The Triumph of American Capitalism*, New York, 1940. On the contemporary problems of American federalism, see my article in the *New Republic*, May 3, 1939.

[183]

of anything like the present economic system means an increasing power in the strong to exploit the weak. Free trade in Europe, for example, could under present conditions have no other effect than to condemn the less developed countries to stabilize their present low standards of life while they supplied the more developed countries with their primary products cheaply; their economic nationalism is the inevitable weapon they have developed to give their industries, and the possibilities they imply, a foothold against the competition of the more developed countries—a foothold, of course, the price of which is borne by the mass of general consumers. Free migration, under these conditions, whether of capital or of labour, means, as before under the present system, the use of lower-paid and unorganized labour to attack the standards it has won so painfully in the better-developed countries; while if, under the normal conditions of a free market, capital from abroad is invested in the expansion of the less developed countries, there develops an economic control of the investing country over its subject—in modern history the classic example is England in Egypt—which, no matter what its efficiency, means all the habits of imperialist expansion.

That is why a vague general will to end sovereignty will find no effective institutional expression unless

we have begun, before victory comes, to end the
vested interests which require sovereignty for their
protection. To be able to have common rules for
the control of those objects by which all of us are
affected, whether they are tariffs or migration, dis-
armament or the labour-standards, we must have an
equal interest in the result of the working of the
common rules; and, frankly, on any short-term view,
say, the life of two generations, there cannot be
that equal interest unless the economic life of the
states concerned to pool their sovereignties is pro-
jected onto a single plane of equality. And there
cannot be that projection in the presence of vested
interests whose life depends upon the maintenance
of inequality. They stand in the way not merely of the
safety of those directly dependent upon them. More
important, they stand in the way of that highroad
to the economics of abundance which alone makes
possible any creative international experiment. For,
unless we end them for this purpose, any attack upon
them is a threat to the well-being of their dependants
in the nation-state they dominate. Given the maintenance of vested interests in Great Britain, our
present economic system means that every extension
of cotton-manufacture in India or Japan is a threat
to employment in Lancashire. On the same assumptions, even, the existence of unorganized masses of
low-paid labour in the Southern states of the United

[185]

States is a threat to the standards of relatively well-organized and well-paid labour in the North. We must never forget that the Civil War came in America essentially because planter capitalism in the South was threatened by the industrial capitalism of the North and could not protect itself against the expansion the latter made possible except by extending its vested interest all over the new economic horizons of the United States; its inability to give way without ruining the owners of the slaves was the root cause of the "irrepressible conflict." And in the same way Fascism must extend all over the world the technique of exploitation it has established in Germany and Italy as the only method at its disposal that is a possible alternative to the economics of abundance. The outlaws guard privilege for their peoples at the expense of sources of well-being that could be opened, even to their victims. They do so because, if those sources of well-being were opened, it would be obvious that the tyranny of the outlaws was superfluous.

I cannot, of course, set out in detail here the kind of organization that is implied in this approach; in any case, too much of the future, even of the immediate future, is concealed from us to make this worth while. I can lay down only certain principles without which, as I conceive, any victory we win will be merely a halting between two wars:

What Are We to Do Next?

1. We must begin now the socialization of those vested interests within Great Britain which, today as in 1918, stand in the way of our surrender of the principle of state-sovereignty.

2. In the building of the new Europe, the socialization of similar interests abroad is essential to the same result.

3. On this basis, it becomes possible to visualize an international organization able to employ in the common interest both the unexploited material sources of wealth and that utilization of them which science makes possible.

4. Such an organization could, in a genuine way, have common rules by which its member-states could be bound, because its distribution of economic power would be the basis of a common interest in their application. Whether the form of organization involved would seek world-wide expression, as in the League of Nations, or whether it should attempt the more modest form of a series of regional systems of states closely linked by territorial contiguity, or whether the second may best be built within the framework of the first, I do not pretend to decide. It seems to me probable that the future form of world government is likely to be more complex than the model of the League led us to imagine; that there are some functions which will require territorial organs operating over a special and rela-

tively narrow area, while others will require *ad hoc* bodies whose power of decision controls all activities universally within the area with which it is concerned.

I do not underestimate the importance of machinery; but machinery is far less important than the basis upon which it rests. I therefore emphasize again that there can be no peace without international organization which abrogates the sovereignty of individual states; no abrogation of sovereignty until we begin to destroy within each state the vested interests which require sovereignty. We cannot solve the problem of peaceful change until we have ended the paradox of poverty in the midst of potential plenty, and we cannot end that paradox until we have effected a massive redistribution of economic power. Peace between states depends upon peace within states; international justice without depends upon social justice within. Leave, as we leave, the profit-making motive its present theatre of operations, and even victory means only the beginning of a new cycle destined to end in a new conflict. Permit the great vested interests—banking, coal, steel, transport, electric power, to take examples only—to treat with the nation-state as independent empires, and they will annex it in the future as they have annexed it in the past. Nothing less than a revolution in the spirit of man is necessary if we are to enter the kingdom of peace as our rightful inheritance; and a revolution in the spirit of man, as all history goes to show, must follow, and cannot precede, a revolution in the relationships of that material world by the exploitation of which he must live.

v

These, I suggest, are the principles with which the British government must approach the peoples whom it seeks to emancipate. With less than these principles any victory it offers them will be as illusory as the Peace of Versailles. For, without them, it may put the defeated in chains; it will yet at every moment fear his escape from those chains. And a generation which, like ours, has known the heavy price of fear cannot afford to make the same mistake a second time.

Fear is the child of privilege; it is endemic in every society where men possess its benefits by the prescription of ancient evil instead of by the justice of an equal interest. To abolish fear, therefore, we need to abolish privilege. We can do it by the voluntary perception of its dangers, or we can do it by the compulsion of violence. If we choose the first way, its basis in the impulse of magnanimity gives us the time to adjust our social order in terms of peace. If we refuse that way, we move relentlessly to that kind of social convulsion in which all the

[189]

worst passions of mankind are loosed. I do not deny
that the way of magnanimity is both hard and rare;
the tradition of privilege is that it persuades its
beneficiaries to transform ancient claims into vested
rights which refuse admission to the pressure of
new claims. I only argue that never has the danger
of their angry maintenance been so clear as in our
day; never, either, has it been so obvious that they
stand in the way of every dream men have dared
to dream.

I have not sought to conceal my view that the
price of victory is a European revolution, for we
cannot unleash the forces that victory requires if
we stand by the ancient ways. Without that revolution both the war and the peace will be no more
than a dispute about the character of a social order
which has twice brought us to world conflict and
will bring us to it again if we seek no more than
its preservation. With that revolution we release
new and immense sources of production which make
possible a different and a better world. It can, as I
have argued, be for ourselves a revolution made
by consent if we have the courage and the imagination to use our opportunities. I have not said that
we shall use them. I have said only that they are
there and that great leadership, which means au-
dacious leadership, need not hesitate to use them.
Certainly no one who has seen the British people

with first-hand intimacy in its hour of supreme danger can doubt that it expects the leadership capable of that audacity.

It will mean sacrifice; it will mean unselfishness; it will mean single-mindedness. I do not deny that it will mean them, and in a high degree. I do not deny, either, that at the parting of the ways between an old civilization and a new these are the rarest of qualities. I have said only that the promise the new civilization implies entitles us to ask for them. For it offers fellowship between men and peace between states upon a basis more sure than in any previous time. It gives us the prospect of planning our lives consciously and in freedom. It gives us access to riches more ample and more justly shared.

Nor is that all. We know, if we are ready to face the facts before us, that the alternative is an age of conflict. We know that hates will multiply, that fears will grow even more profound. We know, also, that the greater the hates, the more profound the fears, the smaller the chance we have of preserving our heritage. We know that the kind of conflict in which, without a revolution by consent, we shall be involved comes to destroy and not to fulfil. It is needless conflict, and it will be the more bitter because those who wage it will know uneasily as they fight that it is a denial, in the evil tradition of the outlaws, of all the nobler impulses of the human

[191]

race. Our choice is between the dark age of privilege and the dawn of an equal fellowship between men. Granted our power to end privilege now, we can build the highroad to that way of living where all men stand, unafraid, in the glad light of freedom. But we must end the rule of privilege speedily lest, amid the clash of arms, we lose the unity of aim which alone gives purpose to the battle.

That is why I have written this book on the assumption that a British victory for these ends is certain; on no other assumption can a free man either think or write today. Nor need he conceal his pride that it is given to his own people to make its victory the primary condition upon which the liberation of all mankind may be built.